DID JESUS RISE FROM THE DEAD?

DID JESUS RISE FROM THE DEAD?

The Resurrection Debate

Gary R. Habermas and Antony G. N. Flew

Edited by Terry L. Miethe

1817

Harper & Row, Publishers, San Francisco

Cambridge, Hagerstown, New York, Philadelphia, Washington
London, Mexico City, São Paulo, Singapore, Sydney

FIRST EDITION

Library of Congress Cataloging-in-Publication Data

Habermas, Gary R.
  Did Jesus rise from the dead?

  Bibliography: p.
  1. Jesus Christ—Resurrection. I. Flew, Antony,
1923– . II. Miethe, Terry L., 1948– .
III. Title.
BT481.H27 1987   232.9'7   85-45355
ISBN 0-06-063549-5

87 88 89 90 91 HC 10 9 8 7 6 5 4 3 2 1

To John-Hayden, Robert, Michelle, Holly, and Kevin
with much love,
in the hope that they will become tough-minded and love the truth

Contents

Part Four: A Final Response

Preface

The Resurrection of Jesus Christ is the most significant topic of our day. Of course Christians since Paul have made that claim, because they have been convinced that it proved Jesus' deity and the efficacy of his death for our sins. The development of the post-Kantian view of religion, however, which now dominates the twentieth century, makes the Resurrection critical in an entirely new way.

In the current view, religion is not an issue of knowledge, of what the facts are, but of faith, of what is believed. This notion of the Resurrection as "existential meaning-making" makes its actual occurrence irrelevant. Further, given the apparently negative results of the great quest for historical proof, the Resurrection is lost to demythologizing. Thus the factuality of the Resurrection is deserted, even by explicitly Christian theologians. Consequently, the very mention of evidence for Jesus' Resurrection is a startling thought. It challenges not only the received evaluation of history but the very nature of religion.

In this context, the debate between Antony G. N. Flew and Gary R. Habermas at Liberty University was perfect staging. Habermas is an expert on the historical evidence, Flew on the impossibility of miracles. They agree that the current view of religion is nonsense—that there is no meaning if there is no event. They agree that the question of the Resurrection must be settled in terms of the sufficiency of the evidence. Finally, they agree that if the Resurrection did occur, then materialism is doomed; there must be a supernatural reality. Thus a true debate was possible, and the reader will discover that it rarely strayed from the central issue: does the evidence demand assent to the historical event? For these reasons I regard this as a crucial and timely book. I hope that it will be a catalyst for further thought that will bring Christian conceptualizing as well as concepts of Christianity back to their factual and historical roots.

I am especially grateful to Professor Terry L. Miethe for initiating and organizing the original debate and also for editing the material into this volume. I am grateful to the staff at Harper & Row, who saw the importance of this project and sent two of their senior staff members to the actual debate. Many others contributed time and energy in making the debate a reality and we in the Department of Philosophy are grateful. Finally, I, with the Department of Philosophy of Liberty University, wish to thank our friend and chancellor for underwriting the expenses of this debate and thus making this book possible.

—W. David Beck
Chairman, Department of Philosophy
Liberty University

Introduction

"Did Jesus rise from the dead? is **the most important** question regarding the claims of the Christian faith. Certainly no question in modern religious history demands more attention or interest, as witnessed by the vast body of literature dealing with the Resurrection.[1] James I. Packer says it well in his response to this debate:

> When Christians are asked to make good their claim that this scheme is truth, they point to Jesus' Resurrection. The Easter event, so they affirm, demonstrated Jesus' deity; validated his teaching; attested the completion of his work of atonement for sin; confirms his present cosmic dominion and his coming reappearance as Judge; assures us that his personal pardon, presence, and power in people's lives today is fact; and guarantees each believer's own reembodiment by Resurrection in the world to come.

The Apostle Paul considered the Resurrection to be the cornerstone of the Christian faith. If Jesus did not rise from the dead, the whole structure, Christianity, collapses. Paul tells us in 1 Corinthians 15:14–17,

> And if Christ has not been raised, *our preaching is useless and so is your faith.* More than that, we are then found to be false witnesses about God. . . . And if Christ has not been raised, *your faith is futile* [emphasis added].

The Christian faith—and its claim to be Truth—exists only if Jesus rose from the dead. The heart of Christianity is a living Christ. "It is in the Risen One that the whole life of mankind ultimately comes to a decision. The ultimate decision, however, is that between life and death. The word of the resurrection of Jesus is the assault of life upon a dying world."[2]

Our debaters echo the importance of the question. Antony G. N. Flew says in his opening remarks in the debate:

> We [Habermas and I] both construe *resurrection,* or rising from the dead, in a thoroughly literal and physical way. . . . We are again agreed that the

question whether, in that literal understanding, Jesus did rise from the dead is of supreme theoretical and practical importance. For the knowable fact that he did, if indeed it is a knowable fact, is the best, if not the only, reason for accepting that Jesus is the God of Abraham, Isaac, and Israel. . . . We are agreed both that that identification is the defining and distinguishing characteristic of the true Christian, and that it is scarcely possible to make it without also accepting that the Resurrection did literally happen.

Having thus established the importance of the question and that the debaters agree on its importance, perhaps a word about how the debate came to be would be appropriate. I have been familiar with Flew's work, especially *God and Philosophy,* since my early days in seminary when a professor of mine required as a term assignment in his Analytic Philosophy class that every student present a critique of Flew's book. It had been my hope, then, for more than fifteen years to see Flew debate the subject of the possibility of miracles, specifically the evidence for the historicity of the Resurrection.

Then in February 1985, Gary R. Habermas and I were invited to participate in a series of debates entitled "Christianity Challenges the University: An International Conference of Theists and Atheists," to be held in Dallas, Texas. The objective of the conference was to present the Christian understanding of reality in the international intellectual community in such a way as to be "forceful and effective as well as intellectually impeccable."[3] This was to be accomplished by inviting renowned scholars in philosophy, the natural sciences, the social sciences, the historical foundations of Christianity, culture, morality, and education to participate in debate via a panel discussion format.

Antony G. N. Flew was one of the panel participants in philosophy to represent the atheist position. After the philosophy panel discussion, Gary R. Habermas and I had dinner with Flew and discussed at length his position regarding the possibility of miracles and the Resurrection of Jesus in particular. It was agreed by Habermas, Flew, and myself that the Resurrection of Jesus presented the most important evidence for the historical reality of miracles. Flew said that he had never adequately addressed this issue in his writings and indicated interest in doing so formally in debate with Habermas and the philosophy faculty of Liberty University.

An invitation to debate "The Historicity of the Resurrection: Did Jesus Rise From the Dead?" was then issued to Flew by the philosophy faculty of Liberty University. Habermas and Flew were to be the primary debaters, with W. David Beck and myself also participating in the discussion. Thus the events that produced the material for this book were a debate of the aforementioned subject by Habermas and Flew held on May 2, 1985, at Liberty University and attended by 3000 people, and a continuation of the debate on May 3, 1985, involving the four of us.

All parties agreed, because of the limitations of time, the demands of the subject, and a belief that the debaters in Dallas had talked past each other to limit the debate to a single issue, that of the historicity of the Resurrection of Jesus. The debate was not to be concerned with issues such as God's existence, revelation (such as the Bible), or miracles in general. These issues could, however, be addressed in the question and answer session following the formal debate.

Because audiences are perennially interested in who the experts choose as the winner of a public debate, we organized two panels of experts in their respective areas of specialty to render a verdict on the present subject matter. One panel consisted of five philosophers, who were instructed to judge the content of the debate and render a winner. The second panel consisted of five professional debate judges, who were asked to judge the argumentation technique of the debaters. All ten participants serve on the faculties of American universities and colleges such as the University of Pittsburgh, the University of Virginia, Western Kentucky University, James Madison University, George Mason University, Randolph-Macon College (Ashland, Virginia), Sweet Briar College, and Liberty University. We attempted to choose persons of a wide spectrum of views and persuasions.

The decisions of our judges were as follows. The panel of philosophers, judging content, cast four votes for Habermas, none for Flew, and one draw. One philosophy judge commented:

I was surprised (shocked might be a more accurate word) to see how weak Flew's own approach was. I expected—if not a new and powerful argument —at least a distinctly new twist to some old arguments. Given the conditions under which public debates are often conducted, many of the finer details of Flew's position do not become evident until the pages of the book that record the dialogue following the public debate [Part Two: The Continuing Debate]. By this time, it becomes clear that even Flew has not rid himself of some of the older, outdated, and discredited objections to the resurrection. When I completed my reading of the debate and the following dialogues, I was left with this conclusion: Since the case against the resurrection was no stronger than that presented by Antony Flew, I would think it was time I began to take the resurrection seriously. My conclusion is that Flew lost the debate and the case for the resurrection won.

Another philosopher commented:

Flew [is defending a point] which he acknowledges to come ultimately from Hume's First Enquiry, that a miracle can never be proved in such a way that it can serve as the foundation for any system of religion. . . . Flew's success in the debate should be measured by how well he came out of it with this claim intact, Habermas's by how well he undermined it. . . . Habermas at first seemed wrongly to interpret Flew to be maintaining a naturalistic bias against the ontological possibility of a miracle. . . . So, Habermas missed the point . . . only if an inconsistency in Flew's position is overlooked. Otherwise, he correctly unearthed the fact that Flew can hold his ground on this point only by maintaining a naturalistic bias against the occurrence of a miracle in spite of his [Flew's] claim not to hold one.

The panel of professional debate judges voted three to two, also in favor of Habermas, this time regarding the method of argumentation technique. One judge noted:

I am of the position that the affirmative speaker [Habermas] has a very significant burden of proof in order to establish his claims. The various historical sources convinced me to adopt the arguments of the affirmative speaker. Dr. Flew, on the other hand, failed, particularly in the rebuttal period and the head-to-head session, to introduce significant supporters of his position. Dr. Habermas placed a heavy burden on Dr. Flew to refute very specific issues. As the rebuttals progressed, I felt that Dr. Flew tried to skirt the charges given him.

Another professional debate judge said:

> I conclude that the historical evidence, though flawed, is strong enough to lead reasonable minds to conclude that Christ did indeed rise from the dead. Habermas has already won the debate. . . . By defeating the Hume-inspired skeptical critique on miracles in general offered by Flew and by demonstrating the strength of some of the historical evidence, Habermas does end up providing "highly probable evidence" for the historicity of the resurrection "with no plausible naturalistic evidence against it." Habermas, therefore, in my opinion, wins the debate.

One of the two professional debate judges who voted for Flew gave the following reason: "Since most debates are decided based upon clash of argument and that characteristic was weak in this debate I hesitate to name a winner. However, given that the request was to name a winner I . . . voted for Professor Flew." And the other debate judge who voted for Flew said: "Flew's strategy is to restrict his argumentative burden to demonstrating the scientific/historical inadequacy of theological explanations of the resurrection stories, rather than proving a contrary explanation. Winner of debate: Flew." This second judge found that Habermas's citations of so many scholars kept him from spending more time on the content of his argument.

The overall decision of the two panels, judging both content and argumentation technique, was a seven to two decision (with one draw) in favor of the historicity of the Resurrection as argued by Habermas. Because of this panel decision, Habermas has been asked to write the reply essay directed to the three internationally known respondents whose perspectives follow the debate sessions.

I am pleased indeed to have three such renowned respondents to the debate. Wolfhart Pannenberg, a German scholar, is one of the world's best-known theologians. Charles Hartshorne, an American philosopher, is the foremost living advocate of process philosophy. James I. Packer, a British scholar, is one of the best-known evangelical theologians of our time. Although we made every possible attempt to find the best-known representative for every scholarly position toward the Resurrection, from evangelical to Catholic to Bultmannian, several scholars were not able to respond because of other commitments.

The decisions regarding the debate should not take the place of a decision from you, the reader. Each person should study the arguments, sift the evidence, and decide which case best fits the facts. This is an area in which the importance of the issue almost invariably involves the emotions, but the question of truth is the initial query. Did Jesus rise from the dead? is what this volume is all about. Of course the issue of the Resurrection of Jesus, which is the subject of the debate, is more important than the personalities involved here. The ideas that constitute this confrontation, and the evidence for them, are the crucial factors before us. The decision is yours. On with the debate!

—Terry L. Miethe
Oxford, England
17 August, 1986

NOTES

1. See the Select Bibliography at the end of this book for examples.
2. Walter Kunneth, *The Theology of the Resurrection* (St. Louis, MO: Concordia, 1965), 295.
3. This is the stated purpose in the bulletin *Christianity Challenges the University: An International Conference of Theists and Atheists* under number 1 of "Objectives."

I. THE FORMAL DEBATE

Negative Statement:
Antony G. N. Flew

I will begin by spelling out three fundamentals upon which Dr. Habermas and I are agreed, notwithstanding that many of those still claiming the Christian name will, nowadays, make so bold as to deny one, or two, or all three of these fundamentals.

First, we both construe *resurrection,* or rising from the dead, in a thoroughly literal and physical way. It is to this understanding that the story of doubting Thomas is so crucially relevant.

Second, we are again agreed that the question whether, in that literal understanding, Jesus did rise from the dead is of supreme theoretical and practical importance. For the knowable fact that he did, if indeed it is a knowable fact, is the best, if not the only, reason for accepting that Jesus is the God of Abraham, Isaac, and Israel.

Third, we are agreed both that that identification is the defining and distinguishing characteristic of the true Christian, and that it is scarcely possible to make it without also accepting that the Resurrection did literally happen. Together these two doctrines constitute what used to be called the scandal of particularity, which would make the discovery of other worlds inhabited by rational moral agents embarrassing to Christianity but not, I think, to any of the other great world religions, and which requires Christians to insist that adherents of all those other religions, and of mine, are, on matters of supreme importance, ruinously wrong.

In these days such fundamentals do need to be reiterated, for sometimes they are denied outright or ignored. Last year, for instance, David Jenkins, a man who has repudiated, and still repudiates, the doctrine of the Resurrection, and that in words too offensive for me to repeat in the presence of genuine believers, was elevated to the senior bishopric of the Church of England. He has since devoted most of his energies

—in the name of the very religion he rejects—to denouncing Margaret Thatcher. This successor to the great Bishop Butler is, alas, not alone in thus surreptitiously replacing Christian faith with socialist activism. The World Council of Churches—so aptly described as UNESCO in clerical dress—and your own National Council of Churches too—both preceded on that fashionable primrose path. Being myself an enemy of socialism, I hesitate to say anything that might persuade Dr. Habermas to jettison his faith!

Our agreement on fundamentals, however, goes only so far. I shall therefore devote the rest of my time to disagreements. My argument falls into two parts: first general, and then particular. The first deals with the general difficulty, perhaps impossibility, of establishing the occurrence of a miracle so as to be the foundation of a system of religion. The second turns to the inadequacies of the evidence actually available in the present case.

Everything that I have to say in general derives ultimately from Hume's first *Enquiry*.[1] But, most emphatically, I shall not be representing what is said there, for that has two major and several lesser faults. Critics such as C. S. Lewis have, quite rightly, made much of some of these.[2]

The first major defect is that by previously denying both natural necessity and natural impossibility, Hume disqualifies himself from distinguishing the genuinely miraculous from the highly unusual or merely marvelous. He thus diminishes the force of his own entirely correct contention that the evidence required to establish the occurrence of the former has to be much stronger than that needed to prove the happening of the latter, just as proof of that demands something rather better than everyday evidence.

The second major defect is that Hume, like most of his contemporaries on both sides of this particular great debate, sees little difference between accusing a witness of perjury and conceding that the testimony of that witness constitutes an accurate account of what actually happened. The truth is that the possibilities of honest error are enormous, especially when the depositions are first recorded long after the alleged events, and without cross-examination of the witnesses; when these alleged events have been much discussed both with other witnesses or supposed witnesses; and when all concerned are trying to fit what actually happened into their own several interpretative frameworks.

The main general argument concerns what, in a landmark paper stimulated by the work of the nineteenth-century German biblical critics, F. H. Bradley called *The Presuppositions of Critical History* (Oxford, 1874). The heart of the matter is that the criteria by which we must assess historical testimony, and the general presumptions that make it possible for us to construe leftovers from the past as historical evidence, are such that the possibility of establishing, on purely historical grounds, that some genuinely miraculous event has occurred is ruled out.

Hume himself concentrated on testimonial evidence because his conception of historiography—later realized in his own best-selling *History of England*—was of a judge assessing, with judicious impartiality, the testimony. This limitation to testimonial evidence is of no immediate consequence to us, although it is worth mentioning that my general argument will not apply, or will not apply without modification, to the Shroud of Turin. That is something that Hume presumably saw in his visit to Turin and, presumably again, would have dismissed as Roman Catholic superstition, happy that in this dismissal all his Protestant contemporaries would agree.

The argument from the presuppositions of critical history embraces three propositions: first, that surviving relics from the past cannot be interpreted as historical evidence, except insofar as we presume that the same fundamental regularities obtained then as still obtain today; second, that in trying to determine what actually happened, historians must employ as criteria all their knowledge of what is probable or improbable, possible or impossible; and third, that because the word *miracle* must be defined in terms of natural necessity and natural impossibility, the application of these criteria inevitably precludes proof of a miracle.

Hume illustrated the first proposition in his *Treatise,* urging that it is only upon such presumptions of regularity that we can justify the conclusion that ink marks on old pieces of paper constitute testimonial evidence.[3] Earlier in the first *Enquiry* he urged the inescapable importance of the criteria demanded by the second. Without criteria there can be no discrimination, and hence no history worthy of the name. What Hume did not and could not bring out was the crucial importance of the notions of natural necessity and natural impossibility, for a strong idea of a natural order is essential if there is to be room for the notion of a miracle as an overriding of that order by a supernatural power. Apologists suggesting that scientists since Einstein have abandoned the search for laws of nature stating physical necessities and physical impossibilities are, therefore, betraying their own cause, and are also mistaken about where science is going.

The practical upshot of all our three methodological contentions, taken together, comes out sharp and clear in a footnote in which Hume quotes with approval the reasoning of the physician De Sylva in the case of Mlle. Thibaut: "It was impossible that she could have been so ill as was 'proved' by witnesses, because it was impossible that she could, in so short a time, have recovered so perfectly as he found her."

That, with regard to the presuppositions of critical history, is the heart of the matter. Confronted with testimonial evidence for the occurrence of a miracle, the secular historian must recognize that however unlikely it may seem that all the witnesses were in error, the occurrence of a genuine miracle is, by definition, naturally impossible. Yet this should not be the end of the affair. For historians, like everyone else, ought to be ever ready, for sufficient reason, to correct their assumptions about what is probable or improbable, possible or impossible. And this readiness should allow that even the qualification *secular* may, for sufficient reason, have to be abandoned.

In defiance of his own principles, Hume insisted that anything that in the Age of Enlightenment he and his colleagues believed to be impossible, was impossible, and that it never could be discovered that any of them had been wrong about impossibilities. So he dismissed stories of two wonders wrought by the Emperor Vespasian, and of several others occurring at the tomb of the Abbé Paris; stories that we now have excellent reason to believe were true. But this, like the appeal to what is supposed to have become the practice of physicists since Einstein is, for the defense of the miraculous, useless. Our reasons for believing that Vespasian did indeed effect two astonishing psychosomatic cures in Egypt are at the same time our reasons for insisting that those cures were not, after all, truly miraculous.

The second point about the need to correct unsound presuppositions is best made by citing Cardinal Newman, who made an unusually strenuous attempt to come to terms with Humean contentions. Newman is prepared to allow the general validity of such principles in the assessment of testimonial evidence. What he challenges is their application to "these particular miracles, ascribed to the particular Peter, James and John. . . ." What has to be asked, Newman continues, is whether they really are "unlikely, supposing that there is a Power, external to the world, who can bring them about; supposing they are the only means by which He can reveal himself to those who need a revelation; supposing that He is likely to reveal himself; that He has a great end in doing so."[4]

Well yes, certainly. If we were in a position to suppose all this, then no doubt the case for the occurrence of these particular miracles, as well as for that of the supreme miracle of the Resurrection, would be open and shut. But those who know all this must already be in possession either of a rich revelation or an unusually abundant natural theology. Given all that, it certainly would be reasonable for them to jettison secular presuppositions, at least in the present context. That, however, is not the situation of those now asked to consider the historical evidence for the Resurrection of Jesus, and this in turn as sufficient reason for identifying Jesus as the God of Mosaic theism.

So much for my general arguments about the presuppositions of critical history. I have tried to show that and explain why purely historical evidence cannot establish the occurrence of any authentic miracle, not, that is, until and unless those presuppositions can be corrected and supplemented, either by a rich and relevant antecedent revelation or by a rich and relevant natural theology. The question now is whether the present case is sufficiently exceptional to require some radical shakeup of secular historiographic presuppositions, either by revising our ideas of what is naturally possible or by admitting that we have a unique and uniquely important case of a supernatural intervention transcending natural impossibilities. To no one's surprise, I am sure, I will argue the negative.

Had I not discredited any such remark in advance by concurring with Hume's contention that we cannot make valid inferences about "the projects and intentions . . . of a Being so different and so much superior," I might have begun my consideration of the evidence in this case by suggesting ways in which a Creator might have been successful in ensuring that everyone received and understood any message that he transmitted. But, of course, any such suggested means might be logically incompatible with the Creator's (naturally) unknown ends. So I have to start with a different employment for Newman's statement.

It serves to remind us of something which, in any examination of the New Testament evidence, we must not forget. This is that Jesus lived among, and preached to, a population that was overwhelmingly Jewish. All the twelve disciples were Jews. All the New Testament converts seem to have been converts to Christianity from Judaism: Paul, for instance, is said to have been raised as a Pharisee. Everyone concerned, therefore, believed in and worshiped the God of Abraham, Isaac, and Israel. They all believed also both that God had in the past sent prophets to the people of the Covenant, the authenticity of whose message had been endorsed by the conspicuous working of miracles, and that there was to be at least one more special man sent from God, the Messiah.

Given these common assumptions, all concerned were eager to interpret their individual experiences within this shared ideological framework. Most important for us is their restless search, both for passages in the Jewish Bible that might be interpreted as prophecies referring to their own time, and for events in that time that could be identified as the fulfillments of such putative prophecies. That this was a practice prevalent in, although by no means peculiar to, that period is abundantly evidenced both inside and outside the New Testament.

In order to indicate how this unfortunate yet entirely honest practice can result in false history, I take as my illustration the shambles of the birth stories.

First, prophecies really did foretell that the Messiah was to be both of the house of David and born in Bethlehem. So if Jesus was indeed the Messiah, he must have been both descended from David and born in Bethlehem. Now, whereas neither Mark nor John suggest any hometown but Nazareth, both Luke and Matthew insist on a birth in Bethlehem. They also provide two totally irreconcilable Davidic genealogies. These disagree even about the name of the grandfather of Jesus. Then, to explain how it was that Mary came to term so far from home, Luke tells the implausible tale of a Roman tax collection census requiring that every householder register not in his or her place of residence, where the taxes were paid, but in his or her birthplace. A Roman census would in any case not have affected Joseph, because in the days of Herod the Great, in which Luke places the birth, neither Galilee nor Bethlehem fell under direct Roman rule.

Second, Matthew and Luke tell us that Mary was at the birth a virgin, whereas neither Mark nor John nor any of the other New Testament writers make this claim. It seems not to occur to either Matthew or Luke that, if true, it would make their Davidic genealogies not only mutually contradictory but also irrelevant. And whereas Luke has the Angel of the Annunciation appear to Joseph, in Matthew the Angel appears to Mary.

Matthew alone is explicit in relating the whole affair to the prophet Isaiah: "Behold, a virgin shall conceive and bear a son, and his name shall be called Emmanuel." But in the original Hebrew, as opposed to the Greek of the Septuagint, the key word is not *betulah* ("virgin") but *almah* ("young woman of marriageable age"). In any case, the context of Isaiah 6:16 makes it clear to the uncommitted reader that the prophecy was intended to refer to a future son of King Ahaz, the later Hezekiah, who lived seven hundred years before Christ. (Perhaps just to tease the prophet, Hezekiah did *not* name the son Emmanuel!)

All this is not the half of it. Yet it should be sufficient to bring out how the search for prophecies and their fulfillments can get in the way of the discovery and the recording of historical truth. The next thing to emphasize is that the earliest written sources still available to us were compiled a long time after the events that they attempt to record. No biblical scholar dates any of the Epistles earlier than the early A.D. 40s, or Mark earlier than the early A.D. 50s, that is to say, roughly ten and roughly twenty years after the Crucifixion, respectively.

By some standards ten or even twenty years is not a long time. Yet it is enough time to permit the forces that corrupt testimony to do irrecoverable damage. Psychic researchers, trying to track down supposed occurrences of what is normally believed to be impossible, would surely regard a case in which there is no hope of finding any contemporary records as unlikely to repay investigation. One does not have to be, though I myself am, sympathetic to Israeli nationalism to regret the decisive suppression of the first century Jewish revolt, for in that destruction of Jerusalem we may well have lost some irreplaceable contemporary records, even perhaps something from some non-Jewish witness of some of the Easter events.

Quite apart from the admitted absence of any truly contemporary documentation of the life and death of Jesus, there is also a lamentable lack of evidence about both the authors and the dates of those compositions that we do have. Perhaps this would not matter if we were dealing with narratives telling of ordinary events. But it most certainly does matter when it is claimed that the four Gospels, with all their apparent inconsistencies and prima facie unbelievabilities, constitute the only accounts of the earthly life, death, and Resurrection of God incarnate.

Nor is it only the crucial documents the dates of which are uncertain. The same uncertainty extends to the dating of all events that they purport to record. What actually happened is, of course, immeasurably more important than when it happened. Nevertheless, if the Gospel writers did think of themselves as writing chronicles of not too remotely past events, then it is odd that they apparently felt no call to give a precise date for any of those events. One incongruous consequence is that Christians, who recognize that their religion is peculiarly historical and who affirm that the events of the original Easter constitute the great hinge of human history, remain unable to specify the year in which these events are supposed to have occurred.

With regard not only to the relatively unimportant matter of the lack of precise dates, but also to wider evidential concerns, two things should be said. First, if the Mosaic God really did reveal himself in Palestine in the early A.D. 30s, then he manifestly did not intend the fact and the contents of that revelation to get through to all humanity and to be accepted by everyone. Second, it is only on the assumption that a genuinely revealing revelation was in fact being made that we become entitled to assume that we now possess evidences sufficient to demand the conclusion that that is the case.

In fact, in view of these and many other deficiencies in the materials available, my own conviction is that we have no chance either of developing a modestly acceptable outline account of what actually happened in Jerusalem during that original Easter weekend, or of determining how or when believers first came to believe that on the third day Jesus physically rose from the dead.

Be that as it may. For in order to warrant disbelief none of that is necessary. It is only sufficient to show that no evidence has been presented so strong as to call for a radical shakeup of the ordinary presuppositions of critical history. We have no alternative but to continue in the presumption that anything that is accepted as being naturally impossible did not happen.

Because so many Christians following St. Paul believe that they can see the risen Christ still active in the lives of believers and in his church, it is worth insisting that to the unsanctified eye, all that is visible here are the effects of the believers' beliefs about the risen Christ. What calls for explanation, therefore, is not these effects themselves, striking and impressive though they often are, but how the believers arrived at the beliefs that produce those effects.

One clue to one possible answer is to be found in what is our earliest testimony about what are alleged to have been post-Resurrection appearances. Most scholars would date this nearer to twenty than to ten years after the Easter events. It is in 1 Corinthians 15. Before looking at this, I must emphasize how much our picture is distorted by reading the books of the New Testament in their traditional order, rather than in order of composition. We falsely assume that the Christ preached by Paul must have been the Jesus of the Gospels. We thus fail to notice that the Pauline epistles contain no references to Pontius Pilate, or to any birth traditions, or to miracles wrought during the ministry of Jesus. Perhaps most remarkable of all, even when these are most relevant to the controversies in which Paul was engaged, they never quote any of the supposedly dominical sayings later to be recorded in the various Gospels.

Thus the Pauline epistles provide no positive support for the assumption, so strongly suggested by the order of books in the New Testament, that the church in Paul's day was familiar with the biographical materials that we now find there. And when we look at his account of post-Resurrection appearances—an account which, though late, is the earliest we have—we have also to remind ourselves that it also may or may not have been available to and accepted by the Gospel writers.

In four successive verses Paul lists first, Cephas (Peter) and the twelve; second, "above five hundred brethren at once"; third, "James, then . . . all the apostles"; and fourth, "last of all he was seen of me also, as of one born out of due time." Nothing is said to indicate where these events are supposed to have occurred, and all that we can infer about when it occurred is that it was after the third day and before Paul's own reception into the Christian community.

Of the Gospels none, not even Matthew, concedes a first appearance to Peter. They have either not heard or not accepted the story of the appearance to "above five hundred brethren at once"—and this despite the "greater part" being still alive at the time of Paul's writing.

Finally, and this is by far the most significant and damaging fact about this earliest testimony, Paul is clearly taking it that his own visionary experience on the road to Damascus was of exactly the same type as all its perceived predecessors. But this vision, like Macbeth's vision of the dagger, was not even alleged to be "sensible to feeling as to sight." It was not, therefore, at all the sort of thing needed by Dr. Habermas, and supposedly, actually vouchsafed to doubting Thomas.

In the rest of the chapter Paul talked of corruption and incorruption and of the provision of spiritual bodies for the resurrected. Presumably he interpreted his own vision on the road to Damascus as seeing Jesus in a nonphysical body. To the unsanctified eye, however, seeing spiritual bodies is indiscernible from having visions to which no mind-independent realities correspond.

NOTES

1. David Hume, *Enquiries Concerning Human Understanding and Concerning the Principles of Morals,* 3rd ed., ed. L. A. Selby-Bigge (Oxford: Clarendon, 1975), 127.
2. C. S. Lewis, *Miracles* (New York: Macmillan, 1947).
3. See Antony G. N. Flew, "Miracles & Methodology" in *Hume's Philosophy of Belief* (London: Routledge and Kegan Paul, 1961).
4. John Henry Cardinal Newman, "Essay on the Miracles Recorded in Ecclesiastical History," in *The Ecclesiastical History of M. L'Abbe Fleury* (Oxford: J. H. Parker, 1842), II (viii) 2, 146.

Affirmative Statement:
Gary R. Habermas

Before turning to the main portion of my presentation, I will begin by noting two limitations. First, Dr. Flew and I have agreed in writing to limit this debate to the historicity of Jesus' Resurrection and not to extend the topic to God's existence, scripture, or other such areas in order to speak directly both on the subject and to each other. Although the Resurrection has implications for these subjects, they are not pursued here. Second, the time element allows me to present only a brief outline of some of the more important evidences for Jesus' Resurrection. Details and additional points will have to await later development, if they can be brought up here at all. Now I will turn directly to my presentation.

First, a few categorical and critical remarks will be addressed to the contemporary philosophical objections to miracles, such as those just presented by Dr. Flew. Second, after a brief treatment of the critically ascertained historical background, four sets of arguments will provide a contemporary apologetic for Jesus' Resurrection. Yet only an outline can be provided here. The strength of this apologetic is in revealing that even by utilizing contemporary critical principles, the Resurrection can still be shown to be historical. In fact, the major theme of this essay is to point out how this event can be demonstrated even according to such skeptical standards of investigation.

CONTEMPORARY PHILOSOPHICAL OBJECTIONS

Frequently following and updating David Hume's influential essay "Of Miracles,"[1] recent philosophical skepticism often focuses on the relationship between miracle-claims[2] and the laws of nature. Some scholars question whether empirical evidence exists for such claims.

Patrick Nowell-Smith, for example, asserts that lawful events are predictable, but nonlawful events are not.[3] Similarly, Antony G. N. Flew[4] and George Chryssides[5] declare that the laws of nature are repeatable, whereas historical claims for miracles are not, and hence the former are more reliable. It is also common to contrast miracle-claims with the laws of nature. Several scholars call for expanding these laws when faced with a strange event.[6] Alasdair McKinnon asserts that all events that occur in nature should be termed natural.[7] Similar views are held by Guy Robinson[8] and Malcolm Diamond.[9] Dr. Flew believes that there is a dilemma between strong laws and real exceptions to these laws.[10]

Because of my time restrictions, I will be able to deal only briefly with these objections, noting five major problems that generally apply to these skeptical doubts. There are numerous individual problems that should be raised with regard to these philosophical questions, which can perhaps be pursued later in our discussion.

First, most of these philosophical objections are attempts to mount up the data against miracles in an a priori manner (that is, before or in spite of the factual evidence) so that no facts could actually establish their occurrence. For instance, it is an unjustified assumption that whatever occurs in the world must automatically be a natural event having a natural cause. Such an assumption ignores the fact that if a historical miracle occurred it would have to occur in nature. Therefore, to always expand the laws of nature belies a naturalistic prejudice.

Searching for a naturalistic alternative may be an expected skeptical procedure, but the statement that we must always assume a naturalistic explanation is, once again, an a priori assumption against miracles. We can describe a natural process but when we attempt to naturalistically predetermine the cause of all events, we beg the very question that we seek to answer, for this is simply another way of assuming that miracles are impossible. As one theistic philosopher remarked concerning Dr. Flew's criticism of miracles, "Flew's argument is an almost classic case of an unfalsifiable position which in the process of justification begs the whole question in favor of naturalism."[11]

Therefore, these naturalistic attempts frequently fail by assuming that which needs to be proven, namely, that all events are indeed natural ones. As C. S. Lewis points out:

> Unfortunately, we know the experience against [miracles] to be uniform only if we know that all reports of them are false. And we can know all the reports to be false only if we know already that miracles have never occurred. In fact, we are arguing in a circle.[12]

We cannot disallow miracles by utilizing faulty definitions, by assuming the evidence needed to prove one's view, or by arguing in a circular fashion. Even while providing a somewhat sympathetic treatment of the naturalistic stance on miracles, another philosopher asserts:

> I believe it is now generally recognized that Hume overstates his case. We cannot a priori rule out the possibility of miracles or of rational belief in miracles. . . . It looks, then, as if Hume's argument against miracles, even as expanded by Flew, fails.[13]

Second, and somewhat conversely, in addition to internal logical problems, these philosophical objections are also mistaken in not allowing for the real possibility of external intervention in nature. But arguing from naturalistic premises inside a system cannot disprove the possibility that a miracle was performed in nature by a stronger power. Therefore, the proper question at this point is not the internal query of the strength of the laws of nature. The more proper question concerns the issue of the supernatural. It should be evident that no matter how strong the natural system is, it is useless to build a case on it if nature is not the supreme reality.[14]

Now it must be noted again that this debate, by agreement, is not about arguments for God's existence and that this is not the issue that I am arguing. Neither am I assuming God's existence or even that a resurrection, by its very nature, is automatically a miracle of God.

Rather, my point is that because the supernatural is at least possible, any claimed evidence for such an event must at least be seriously considered, for if there is even possible evidence for a supernatural act it would make a strong claim to being evidence that is superior to our current evidence regarding the laws of nature.

Third, these philosophical objections generally treat the laws of nature in an almost Newtonian sense as the final word on what may occur. But these objections too often exhibit little awareness of the current view in physics that the laws of nature are statistical. That is, these laws describe what generally occurs. But laws do not cause or keep anything from happening.[15] As a result, these laws should not be utilized as any sort of barrier to the occurrence of miracles. Richard Swinburne points out that the concept of universal, fixed laws reigned from the eighteenth to the early twentieth centuries, but the statistical concept is more recent and popular today.[16] For reasons such as these, eminent German physicist Werner Schaaffs concludes that "even the physicist must officially concede the possibility of intervention by God."[17] Swinburne adds:

> For these latter reasons it seems not unnatural to describe E as a non-repeatable counter-instance to a law of nature L. . . . To say that a certain such formula is a law is to say that in general its predictions are true and that any exceptions to its operation cannot be accounted for by another formula which could be taken as a law. . . . It is clearly a coherent way of talking. . . . In such a case the conceptually impossible would occur.[18]

Therefore, we may make a general point here. If the laws of nature are represented as inviolable then a question-begging assumption occurs when the evidence for Jesus' Resurrection is ignored, as is often the case. But if these laws are general and statistical, then there is no problem for miracles. There are other options besides these two opposite views, but the treatment of them generally falls into such categories.

Very briefly, a fourth issue concerns the empirical bias of several of the philosophical objections to miracles. Strict empiricism ignores both the empirical (even repeatable) evidence for miracles and the fact that the strict forms of verificational standards are themselves nonverifiable. In other words, to require repeatable, empirical evidence as the only or major epistemological test for truth sets up criteria that are themselves nonempirical and that rule out, a priori, vast ranges of reality. Miracles cannot be ruled out by this method because the methodology rules itself out in the process.[19] Such is the case, for instance, with the claims of Drs. Flew and Chryssides that miracles are questionable because of their nonrepeatable nature. This charge may be dealt with more fully in the rebuttal periods.

Fifth and last, the philosophical approach mentioned here frequently ignores the strong historical evidence for the Resurrection of Jesus. Theists are often requested to provide such evidence; it should not be ignored or ruled out a priori when it is given.

For these and many other reasons, such philosophical objections to miracles cannot rule out the historical evidence for the Resurrection, to which we now turn. This evidence must be answered directly on its own grounds.

THE KNOWN HISTORICAL FACTS

Just before turning to an apologetic for the Resurrection, it should be mentioned that the critical approach to this topic has changed substantially in recent decades. The naturalistic theories of the nineteenth-century older liberal theologians are rarely held these days, as will be mentioned in the next section. Rather, by historical investigation or by the utilization of form and redaction criticism, contemporary scholars have approached this event in a different manner. Even by these critical methodologies, a substantial number of historical facts are accepted with regard to the death and Resurrection of Jesus.

Some events are generally agreed to be facts by practically all critical scholars who deal with this topic today, whatever their school of thought or discipline. In other words, critical historians, philosophers, theologians, and scripture scholars who address this subject usually accept this factual basis. At least eleven events are considered to be knowable history by virtually all scholars, and a twelfth event is considered to be knowable history by many scholars.

(1) Jesus died due to the rigors of crucifixion and (2) was buried. (3) Jesus' death caused the disciples to despair and lose hope. (4) Although not as frequently recognized, many scholars hold that Jesus was buried in a tomb that was discovered to be empty just a few days later.

Critical scholars even agree that (5) at this time the disciples had real experiences that they believed were literal appearances of the risen Jesus.

Because of these experiences, (6) the disciples were transformed from doubters who were afraid to identify themselves with Jesus to bold proclaimers of his death and Resurrection, even being willing to die for this belief. (7) This message was central in the early church preaching and (8) was especially proclaimed in Jerusalem, where Jesus had died shortly before.

As a result of this message, (9) the church was born and grew, (10) with Sunday as the primary day of worship. (11) James, the brother of Jesus and a skeptic, was converted to the faith when he also believed he saw the resurrected Jesus. (12) A few years later Paul the persecutor of Christians was also converted by an experience that he, similarly, believed to be an appearance of the risen Jesus.

These historical facts are crucial to a contemporary investigation of Jesus' Resurrection. Except for the empty tomb, virtually all critical scholars who deal with this issue agree that these are the minimum known historical facts regarding this event. Any conclusion concerning the historicity of the Resurrection should therefore properly account for this data. The pivotal fact, recognized as historical by virtually all scholars, is the original experiences of the disciples. It is nearly always admitted that the disciples had actual experiences and that something really happened. Interestingly, varying critical positions that support the literal facticity of Jesus' Resurrection are currently popular.

A CONTEMPORARY APOLOGETIC

NATURALISTIC THEORIES

We will now begin our apologetic for Jesus' Resurrection, supported by four major sets of arguments. First, naturalistic theories have failed to explain away this event, chiefly because each theory is disproven by the known historical facts, as are combinations of theories.[20] Perhaps one or more such theories can be pursued later in the discussion.

One interesting illustration of this failure of the naturalistic theories is that they were disproven by the nineteenth-century older liberals themselves, by whom these theses were popularized. These scholars refuted each other's theories, leaving no viable naturalistic hypotheses.

For instance, Albert Schweitzer dismissed Reimarus's fraud theory and listed no proponents of this view since 1768.[21] David Strauss delivered the historical death blow to the swoon theory held by Karl Venturini, Heinrich Paulus, and others.[22] On the other hand, Friedrich Schleiermacher and Paulus pointed out errors in Strauss's hallucination theory. The major decimation of the hallucination theory, however, came at the hands of Theodor Keim.[23] Otto Pfleiderer was critical of the legendary or mythological theory, even admitting that it did not explain Jesus' Resurrection.[24] By these critiques such scholars pointed out that each of these theories was disproven by the historical facts.

Although nineteenth-century liberals decimated each other's views individually, twentieth-century critical scholars have generally rejected naturalistic theories as a whole, judging that they are incapable of explaining the known data. This approach is a usual characteristic of recent schools of thought.

For instance, Karl Barth points out that each of these liberal hypotheses is confronted by many inconsistencies and he concludes that "today we rightly turn up our nose at this."[25] Raymond Brown likewise asserts that twentieth-century critical scholars have rejected these theories, holding that they are no longer respectable. He adds that such contemporary thinkers ignore these alternative views and any popularized renditions of them as well.[26] In addition to Barth and Brown, rejections come from such diverse critical scholars as Paul Tillich,[27] Wolfhart Pannenberg,[28] Günther Bornkamm,[29] Ulrich Wilckens,[30] John A. T. Robinson,[31] and A. M. Hunter,[32] among others. That even such critical scholars have rejected these naturalistic theories is a significant epitaph for the failure of these views. Perhaps Dr. Flew would like to pursue one or more of these hypotheses later.

EVIDENCES FOR THE RESURRECTION

The second set of arguments in our apologetic for Jesus' Resurrection concerns the many positive evidences that corroborate the historical and literal nature of this event. Ten such evidences will be listed here, all of which have been taken from the accepted historical facts previously listed. Thus, the factual basis for these evidences is admitted by the vast majority of scholars. Because of the brevity of this essay, these ten will simply be stated with very little elaboration.

The key evidence for Jesus' Resurrection is (1) the disciples' eyewitness experiences, which they believed to be literal appearances of the risen Jesus; these experiences have not been explained by naturalistic theories and additional facts corroborate this eyewitness testimony. Other positive evidences include (2) the early proclamation of the Resurrection by these eyewitnesses, (3) their transformation into bold witnesses who were willing to die for their convictions, (4) the empty tomb, and (5) the fact that the Resurrection of Jesus was the center of the apostolic message, all of which require adequate explanations. It is also found that the disciples proclaimed this message in Jerusalem itself, where it is related that in repeated confrontations with the authorities, (6) the Jewish leaders could not disprove their message even though they had both the power and the motivation to do so.

Additionally, (7) the very existence of the church, founded by monotheistic, law-abiding Jews who nonetheless (8) worshiped on Sunday demand historical causes as well.

Two additionally strong facts arguing for the historicity of the Resurrection are that two skeptics, (9) James and (10) Paul, became Christians after having experiences that they also believed were appearances of the risen Jesus. It is interesting to note here that Reginald Fuller concludes that even if the appearance to James had not been recorded by Paul (1 Cor. 15:7), such would still have to be postulated anyway in order to account for both James's conversion and his subsequent promotion to an authoritative position in the early church.[33] The same is even more emphatically true concerning Paul.[34]

When combined with the failure of both the naturalistic theories and the philosophical objections, this minimum of ten evidences provides a strong case for the historicity of Jesus' Resurrection. This is especially so in that each of these evidences was based on a known historical fact.[35] In particular, when the early and eyewitness experiences of the disciples, James, and Paul are considered, along with their corresponding transformations and their central message,[36] the historical Resurrection becomes the best explanation for the facts, especially because the alternative theories have failed. Therefore, it may be concluded that the

Resurrection is a probable historical event. An additional two sets of arguments will now be given to further strengthen this case.

THE CORE HISTORICAL FACTS

The pivotal point in this discussion is the cause of the disciples' faith. As noted by Fuller:

The very fact of the church's kerygma therefore requires that the historian postulate some other event over and above Good Friday, an event which is not itself the "rise of the Easter faith" but the *cause* of the Easter faith. (italics added)[37]

In examining the cause of the disciples' faith, I pointed out earlier that the Resurrection was proclaimed by the earliest eyewitnesses. This is especially based, for instance, on 1 Cor. 15:3ff., where virtually all scholars agree that Paul recorded an ancient creed concerning Jesus' death and Resurrection. That this material is traditional and pre-Pauline is evident from the technical terms *delivered* and *received,* the parallelism and somewhat stylized content, the proper names of Cephas and James, the non-Pauline words, and the possibility of an Aramaic original.[38]

Concerning the date of this creed, critical scholars almost always agree that it has a very early origin, usually placing it in the A.D. 30s. Paul most likely received this material during his first visit in Jerusalem with Peter and James, who are included in the list of appearances (1 Cor. 15:5, 7).[39] In fact, Fuller,[40] Hunter,[41] and Pannenberg[42] are examples of critical scholars who date Paul's receiving of this creed from three to eight years after the Crucifixion itself. And if Paul received it at such an early date, the creed itself would be even earlier because it would have existed before the time he was told. And the facts upon which the creed was originally based would be earlier still. We are, for practical purposes, back to the original events. So we may now realize how this data is much earlier than the ten to twenty years after the Crucifixion as postulated by Dr. Flew. Paul also adds that the other eyewitnesses had likewise been testifying concerning their own appearances of the risen Jesus (1 Cor. 15:11, 14, 15).

That these eyewitnesses are said both to have seen the risen Jesus (the creed, 1 Cor. 15:3ff.) and to have testified concerning these experiences (vv. 11, 14–15) is important, for here are two invaluable sources of testimony that link the Resurrection appearances to the earliest eyewitnesses who actually participated in the events.

For the original eyewitnesses, their experiences were literal appearances of the risen Jesus. As explained by Carl Braaten:

> Even the more skeptical historians agree that for primitive Christianity . . . the resurrection of Jesus from the dead was a real event in history, the very foundation of faith, and not a mythical idea arising out of the creative imagination of believers.[43]

In speaking of the nature of these experiences, it is common to stress the descriptions of Paul's experience on the road to Damascus.[44] Yet even critics also recognize the fact that the Gospels likewise contain some early material concerning the Resurrection appearances of Jesus. For instance, Luke 24:34 is believed to be based on tradition perhaps as early as that of the creed recorded by Paul (1 Cor. 15:3ff.). Contrary to Dr. Flew's statement, the appearance to Peter (listed by Paul) is recorded in Luke and is also an early creed, as even Bultmann attests.[45]

After applying form critical techniques to the Gospels, C. H. Dodd shows that the Gospels contain several reports of the resurrected Jesus that rely on early tradition. He cites the appearances recorded in Matthew 28:8–10, 16–20, John 20:19–21, and, to a lesser extent, Luke 24:36–49 as being based on such early tradition. He states, however, that the other Gospel accounts lack the mythical tendencies of much ancient literature and thus also merit careful consideration in a formulation of the appearances of the risen Jesus. At any rate, the Gospel accounts of the Resurrection appearances (and the earliest reports included in them, in particular) should be utilized as records of what the eyewitnesses actually saw.[46] For reasons such as these, many, if not most, critical theologians hold either that the literal event of the Resurrection can be accepted by faith or that some sort of literal appearances (abstract or bodily) may be postulated as historical realities.[47]

Although it is beyond the limits of this essay to attempt to describe the actual characteristics of Jesus' Resurrection body, it may be stated that the combined testimony of the New Testament is that Jesus rose bodily, but that this body was changed.[48] This is the report of the earliest eyewitnesses.

Twelve events were enumerated earlier, eleven of which are accepted as knowable history by virtually all scholars, and one of which is accepted as knowable history by many scholars. It is this writer's conviction that by utilizing only four of these accepted facts, a brief but sufficient case can be made for the historicity of the Resurrection, which will provide a third major set of arguments for this event. (These core facts are only an example of such an argument. If one feels that they are too brief, one only needs to utilize more of the Known Historical Facts enumerated earlier.) The four facts to be used here are Jesus' death due to crucifixion, the subsequent experiences that the disciples were convinced were literal appearances of the risen Jesus, the corresponding transformation of these men, and Paul's conversion experience, which he also believed was an appearance of the risen Jesus. Few scholars dispute these four facts.[49]

Of these facts, the nature of the disciples' experiences is the most crucial. As eminent historian Michael Grant asserts, historical investigation actually does prove that the earliest eyewitnesses were absolutely convinced they had seen the risen Jesus.[50] Carl Braaten adds that skeptical historians in general agree with this conclusion.[51] One major advantage of these critically accepted historical facts is that they deal directly with the issue of these experiences. These four historical facts are able, on a smaller scale, to both provide a few major refutations of the naturalistic theories and to provide some major positive evidences that relate the historicity of Jesus' literal Resurrection, as claimed by the New Testament authors.[52] A few examples will now illustrate these claims.

First, using these four core historical facts, the naturalistic theories can be disproven. (Of course, nothing near an exhaustive set of critiques can be supplied by these facts alone, yet some of the best criticisms do come from this list.) For instance, the swoon theory is ruled out both by the facts concerning Jesus' death and by Paul's conversion. The disciples' experiences disprove the hallucination and other subjective theories because such phenomena are not collective or contagious, being observed by one person alone and taking place at a wide variety of times and places. The psychological preconditions for hallucinations are also lacking. Paul's experience also rules out these theories because of his psychological frame of mind. That it was the disciples and other early witnesses who had these experiences likewise rules out legend or mythological theories, because the original teaching concerning the Resurrection is therefore based on the testimony of real eyewitnesses (as with the creed in 1 Cor. 15:3ff.) and not on later legends. Paul's experience likewise cannot be explained by legends, because such could not account for his conversion from skepticism. Last, the stolen body and fraud theories are disproven by the disciples' transformation, both because this change shows that the disciples really believed that Jesus rose from the dead and because of the probability that a group of such liars would not be willing to become martyrs. Similarly, Paul would not have been convinced by such fraud.[53]

Second, these four core facts also provide the major positive evidences for Jesus' literal Resurrection appearances, such as the disciples' early, eyewitness experiences that have not been explained away naturalistically, their transformation into men who were willing to die specifically for their faith, and Paul's experience and corresponding transformation. Thus these accepted core historical facts provide positive evidences that further verify the disciples' claims concerning Jesus' literal Resurrection, especially in that these arguments have not been accounted for naturally.[54]

But here is the major point of this argument. Because these core historical facts (and the earlier known facts in general) have been established by critical and historical procedures, contemporary scholars should not reject this evidence simply by referring to "discrepancies" in the New Testament or to its general "unreliability." Not only are such critical claims refuted by evidence not discussed here, but it has been concluded that the Resurrection can be historically demonstrated even when the minimum number of historical facts are utilized. Neither should it be concluded merely that something occurred that is indescribable because of naturalistic premises, or because of the character of history, or because of the "cloudiness" or "legendary character" of the New Testament. Neither should it be said that Jesus rose spiritually, but not literally. Again, these and other such views are refuted in that the facts admitted by virtually all scholars as knowable history are adequate to historically demonstrate the literal Resurrection of Jesus.

In short, instead of stating what they believe we cannot know concerning the Gospel accounts, skeptics would do well to concentrate on what even they admit can be known about the texts at this point. The factual basis is enough to vindicate the various accounts and show that Jesus' Resurrection is by far the best historical explanation. Although critical doubts may be present with regard to other issues in the New Testament, the known facts (see The Known Historical Facts) are sufficient to show that Jesus rose from the dead.[55]

THE SHROUD OF TURIN

The fourth set of arguments for the Resurrection of Jesus concerns the scientific investigation of the Shroud of Turin, the results of which can be treated here in only a sketchy manner. I coauthored a book on the shroud with Kenneth Stevenson, who served as the editor and spokesperson for the scientists who investigated the shroud in 1978. I'll refer the interested person to his work or other good books on the subject.[56]

The shroud is a piece of linen that bears the image of a crucified man who has all of the wounds associated with Jesus' death, including a pierced scalp, a serious beating, contusions on the knees and shoulders, four nail wounds in the wrists and feet, as well as a postmortem blood flow from a chest wound. The man is in a state of rigor mortis, another evidence of death.

The man has been identified as a Semite, and evidence from coins over the eyes, pollen, and numerous historical references connect the shroud with a likely first-century origin.[57] But not only do the wounds on the cloth parallel those of Jesus, but they do so in more than a half-dozen areas that are unusual for a crucifixion. Several scientific researchers have noted the high probability that the two men are the same person, based largely on these agreements in rare and abnormal aspects.[58] As even an agnostic scientific critic of the shroud asserts concerning these probabilities in *The Skeptical Inquirer:* "I agree . . . on all of this. If the shroud is authentic, the image is that of Jesus."[59] In other words, this agnostic researcher asserts that if the shroud is not a fake, then it is Jesus' burial cloth.

But perhaps the strongest major conclusion emerging from the investigation is that the shroud is authentic. As one official scientific report states: "No pigments, paints, dyes or stains have been found on the fibrils."[60] Equally intriguing, scientific discoveries concerning the shroud, such as its three-dimensionality, superficiality, and nondirectionality are virtually unexplainable in current scientific terms.[61]

Further, there is no bodily decomposition on the shroud, indicating the separation of the body from the cloth. Additionally, the scientific team's chief pathologist has testified that although the body exited, it was probably not unwrapped, as indicated by the condition of the blood stains. Kenneth Stevenson and I, as well as others, have argued that the evidence indicates the probable cause of the image on the cloth to be a light or heat scorch from a dead body.

In fact, the shroud image appears to be a type of photographic negative, caused by heat or light, having the unique empirical and repeatable characteristics previously mentioned, all proceeding from a dead body and possibly even picturing the body leaving the cloth without being unwrapped. But more than an indescribable mystery, when combined with the probable identification of the shroud as Jesus' burial garment, the shroud becomes an additional set of arguments for Jesus' Resurrection. It should be noted that scientific data can change, and nothing in the Christian faith depends on the shroud (unlike the other three sets of arguments). Yet the evidence at present provides some empirically repeatable evidence for the Resurrection.[62]

CONCLUSION

When one assumes a viewpoint or theory in advance of the data in order to arrive at a conclusion and continues to do so in spite of contrary evidence, one is guilty of a priori reasoning. Continued refusals to seriously consider the facticity of such claims in light of extremely strong evidence while generally ignoring the evidence itself is an example of an a priori (and circular) rejection. I therefore encourage Dr. Flew to address himself to the evidence for the Resurrection.

To be more specific, I would respectfully challenge Dr. Flew to answer evidence for the Resurrection, namely, the failure of the naturalistic theories, the positive evidences for this event, the core facts accepted by virtually all scholars, and the Shroud of Turin. The evidence shows that the claims of the earliest eyewitnesses have been vindicated—Jesus' literal Resurrection from the dead in a glorified, spiritual body is the best explanation for the facts. Dr. Flew, please *directly* address the evidence for the Resurrection in your rebuttal.

NOTES

1. David Hume, *An Enquiry Concerning Human Understanding*, section 10.
2. I make a distinction here between miracles and miracle-claims because demonstrating the former involves God's actual existence and is hence beyond the agreed scope of this debate. For an apologetic that argues from Jesus' Resurrection to God's existence and theology, see Gary R. Habermas, *The Resurrection of Jesus: An Apologetic* (Grand Rapids, MI: Baker Book House, 1980; Lanham, MD: University Press of America, 1984).
3. Patrick Nowell-Smith, "Miracles," in *New Essays in Philosophical Theology*, ed. Antony Flew and Alasdair MacIntyre (New York: Macmillan, 1955), 251–253.
4. *The Encyclopedia of Philosophy*, s.v. "miracles," Antony Flew, 350, 352.
5. George Chryssides, "Miracles and Agents," *Religious Studies* 11 (September 1975): 319–327.
6. For instances, see Antony Flew, *Hume's Philosophy of Belief* (London: Routledge and Kegan Paul, 1961), 193, 201; David Basinger, "Christian Theism and the Concept of Miracle: Some Epistemological Perplexities," *The Southern Journal of Philosophy*, 28 (Summer 1980): 137–150.
7. Alasdair McKinnon, " 'Miracle' and 'Paradox'," *American Philosophical Quarterly* 4 (1967): 309, for instance.
8. Guy Robinson, "Miracles," *Ratio* 9 (December 1967): 155–166.
9. Malcolm Diamond, "Miracles," *Religious Studies* 9 (September 1973): 320–321.
10. *Encyclopedia of Philosophy*, s.v. "miracles," Flew, 347; s.v. Flew, 202.
11. Norman Geisler, *Christian Apologetics* (Grand Rapids, MI: Baker Book House, 1976), 269.
12. C. S. Lewis, *Miracles* (New York: Macmillan, 1947), 105.
13. Stephen T. Davis, "Is It Possible to Know That Jesus Was Raised From the Dead?," *Faith and Philosophy* 1 (April 1984): 148, 150.
14. Lewis, *Miracles*, 106.
15. Werner Schaaffs, *Theology, Physics and Miracles*, trans. Richard Renfield (Washington, DC: Canon Press, 1974), 55, 65, for instance.
16. Richard Swinburne, *The Concept of Miracle* (New York: Macmillan and St. Martin, 1970), 2–3.
17. Schaaffs, *Theology, Physics and Miracles*, 66.
18. Swinburne, *The Concept of Miracles*, 27–28.

19. For some similar ideas, see David Elton Trueblood, *Philosophy of Religion* (New York: Harper & Brothers, 1957), 195–202.

20. It is impossible in the scope of this essay to deal with each of these naturalistic theories and their refutations. For details, see Gary Habermas, *The Resurrection of Jesus: A Rational Inquiry* (Ann Arbor; MI: University Microfilms, 1976), especially 114–171.

21. Albert Schweitzer, *The Quest of the Historical Jesus*, trans. W. Montgomery (New York: Macmillan, 1968), 21–23.

22. David Strauss, *A New Life of Jesus*, vol. 1 (London: Williams and Norgate, 1879), 412; see also Albert Schweitzer's assertion that Strauss administered the death blow to such rationalistic thought, Schweitzer, *Quest of Jesus*, 56.

23. Friedrich Schleiermacher, *The Christian Faith*, vol. 2, ed. H. R. Mackintosh and J. S. Stewart (New York: Harper & Row, 1963), 420; Schweitzer, *Quest of Jesus*, 54–55; 211–214. James Orr, *The Resurrection of Jesus* (Grand Rapids, MI: Zondervan, 1965), 219.

24. Otto Pfleiderer, *Early Christian Conception of Christ* (London: Williams and Norgate, 1905), 152–159.

25. Karl Barth, *The Doctrine of Reconciliation*, vol. 4, part 1 of *Church Dogmatics*, ed. G. W. Bromiley and T. F. Torrance (Edinburgh, Scotland: T. and T. Clark, 1956), 340.

26. Raymond Brown, "The Resurrection and Biblical Criticism," *Commonweal* 87, (November 24, 1967): especially 233.

27. Paul Tillich, *Systematic Theology*, vol. 2 (Chicago: University of Chicago Press, 1971), especially 156.

28. Wolfhart Pannenberg, *Jesus—God and Man*, trans. Lewis L. Wilkens and Duane Priebe (Philadelphia: Westminster Press, 1968), 88–97.

29. Günther Bornkamm, *Jesus of Nazareth*, trans. Irene and Fraser McLuskey with James M. Robinson (New York: Harper & Row, 1960), 181–185.

30. Ulrich Wilckens, *Resurrection*, trans. A. M. Stewart (Edinburgh, Scotland: Saint Andrews Press, 1977), 117–119.

31. John A. T. Robinson, *Can We Trust the New Testament?* (Grand Rapids, MI: Eerdmans, 1977), 123–125.

32. A. M. Hunter, *Bible and Gospel* (Philadelphia: Westminster Press, 1969), 111.

33. Fuller, *The Formation of the Resurrection Narratives* (New York: Macmillan, 1971), 37.

34. *Ibid.*, 37, 46–47.

35. As mentioned earlier, this is, with the exception of the empty tomb, accepted by many recent scholars as historical. See Robert H. Stein, "Was the Tomb Really Empty?" *Journal of the Evangelical Theological Society* 20:1 (March 1977): 23–29.

36. This does not even include the experience of the more than five hundred people who claimed to have seen the risen Jesus and concerning whom Paul asserted that most were still alive and therefore could be questioned.

37. Fuller, *Resurrection Narratives*, 169; cf. Robinson, "Miracles," 124–125.

38. See especially Joachim Jeremias, *The Eucharistic Words of Jesus*, trans. Norman Perrin (London: SCM Press, 1966), 101–103; Fuller, *Resurrection Narratives*, Chapter Two, among others.

39. Oscar Cullmann, *The Early Church*, ed. A. J. B. Higgins (Philadelphia: Westminster Press, 1966), 65–66; C. H. Dodd, *The Apostolic Preaching and Its Developments* (Grand Rapids, MI: Baker Book House, 1980), 16; Raymond Brown, *The Virginal Conception*

and Bodily Resurrection of Jesus (New York: Paulist Press, 1973), 81; George E. Ladd, *I Believe in the Resurrection of Jesus* (Grand Rapids, MI: Eerdmans, 1975), 142, 161; Gerald O'Collins, *What Are They Saying About the Resurrection?* (New York: Paulist Press, 1978), 112.

40. Fuller, *Resurrection Narratives*, 48.

41. A. M. Hunter, *Jesus: Lord and Saviour* (Grand Rapids, MI: Eerdmans, 1976), 100.

42. Pannenberg, *Jesus—God and Man*, 90.

43. Carl Braaten, *History and Hermeneutics*, vol. 2 of *New Directions in Theology Today*, ed. William Hordern (Philadelphia: Westminster Press, 1966), 78.

44. See Acts 9:1–7, 22:5–11, and 26:12–18; 1 Corinthians 9:1, 15:8.

45. For instance, Jeremias, *The Eucharistic Words of Jesus*, 306; Rudolf Bultmann, *Theology of the New Testament*, vol. 1, trans. Kendrick Grobel (New York: Scribner, 1951, 1955), 45; Brown, *Virginal Conception*, 93.

46. C. H. Dodd, "The Appearances of the Risen Christ: An Essay in Form-Criticism of the Gospels," in *More New Testament Studies* (Grand Rapids, MI: Eerdmans, 1968).

47. Gary R. Habermas, "Jesus' Resurrection and Contemporary Criticism: An Apologetic" (Paper delivered at the Evangelical Philosophical Society national meeting, Essex Fells, New Jersey, December 16, 1982). Cf. O'Collins, "Models of the Resurrection" in *What Are They Saying?*

48. Brown, "The Resurrection and Biblical Criticism," 235–236.

49. For a sampling of those who accept the historicity of these facts, see Bultmann, *Theology of the New Testament*, 44–45; Paul Tillich, *Systematic Theology*, 153–158; Bornkamm, *Jesus*, 179–186; Wilckens, *Resurrection*, 112–113; Fuller, *Resurrection Narratives*, 27–49; Pannenberg, *Jesus—God and Man*, 88–106; Brown, *The Virginal Conception*, 81–92; Jürgen Moltmann, *Theology of Hope*, trans. James W. Leitch (New York: Harper & Row, 1967), 197–202; Hunter, *Jesus: Lord and Saviour*, 98–103; Norman Perrin, *The Resurrection According to Matthew, Mark and Luke* (Philadelphia: Fortress Press, 1977), 78–84; Paul Van Buren, *The Secular Meaning of the Gospel* (New York: Macmillan, 1963), 126–134.

50. Michael Grant, *Jesus: An Historian's Review of the Gospels* (New York: Scribner, 1977), especially 176.

51. Braaten, *History and Hermeneutics*, 78.

52. See Gary R. Habermas, "Primary Sources: Creeds and Facts" in *Ancient Evidence for the Life of Jesus: Historical Records of His Death and Resurrection* (Nashville: Nelson, 1984) for this argument in expanded form, including support of these facts.

53. *Ibid.* Expansions of these critiques and many additional ones gathered from the accepted historical facts with regard to these and other such theories cannot be presented here. For a more complete treatment, see Habermas, *The Resurrection of Jesus: A Rational Inquiry*, 114–171.

54. The additional accepted facts enumerated earlier provide other significant arguments for this event, such as the other six evidences previously listed.

55. See Habermas, *Ancient Evidence for the Life of Jesus*, 129–132.

56. For details, see Kenneth E. Stevenson and Gary R. Habermas, *Verdict on the Shroud: Evidence for the Death and Resurrection of Jesus* (Ann Arbor, MI: Servant Books, 1981; Wayne, PA: Dell, 1982); John Heller, *Report on the Shroud of Turin* (Boston: Houghton Mifflin, 1983).

57. See Stevenson and Habermas, "The Shroud and History" in *Verdict on the Shroud.*

58. *Ibid.,* "The Man Buried in the Shroud" and "Is It Jesus?" Cf. Vincent J. Donovan, "The Shroud and the Laws of Probability," *The Catholic Digest* (April 1980): 49–52.

59. Steven D. Schafersman, "Science, The Public, and the Shroud of Turin," *The Skeptical Inquirer* 6 (Spring 1982): 41.

60. Shroud of Turin Research Project (STRP), "Text," New London, CT (October 1981), 1.

61. See Stevenson and Habermas, "Science and the Shroud" in *Verdict on the Shroud.*

62. *Ibid.,* "The Resurrection of Jesus: New Evidence." Stevenson and I do not presume to speak for others in our conclusions.

Rebuttal: Antony G. N. Flew

Well, yes, let's try to do it. Dr. Habermas asked me whether I was an adherent of the swoon theory or any of these other accounts. No, I am not. My argument is that we are simply not in a position to reconstruct an account. I think the whole exercise of who moved the stone and so on is an impossible and misguided exercise because we have not got enough evidence of what actually happened in that undated year of the Easter events.

And the sort of thing that one would like to have, I think, is the sort of thing that might have existed, but if it did, would have been destroyed during the destruction of Jerusalem. One of the reasons, apart from sympathy with Israeli nationalism, for regretting the defeat of the first Jewish rebellion is that the destruction of Jerusalem destroyed any records that the Roman authorities may have had. And the sort of thing I would like to see is the sort of account that a British colonial civil servant would have written of the case. Something such as, "Had an impossible Jewish fanatic to deal with. Do you know the man claimed to be the local god? Good heavens!" That sort of thing, or something from the Jewish authorities about the difficulties they had. All this talk about how we know that the Jewish authorities tried to suppress the evidence and they weren't able to conceal the thing. What we've actually got is statements written down a very long time after those events saying that this is what the Jewish authorities did.

Let me go on to this thing about my, as I thought, generous statement about ten or, in the other case, twenty years as a minimum estimate. I was not referring to the date of Paul's experience on the road to Damascus but to the presumed earliest date of 1 Corinthians, when he wrote it down. And I was also taking it, and I wasn't making it 10 or 20 A.D., I meant ten or twenty years after the estimated date of the Easter events, which is roughly 30 A.D., isn't it—this is the agreed date. So I was taking it that the minimum estimate for the date of

1 Corinthians would be, say, 40 A.D., ten years after the event, which is a long time in the context of psychic research. Anyone who knows anything of the literature in that field would recognize that if your earliest written testimony of some alleged event was ten years later, most people in the field would say, "This is just hopeless. We cannot possibly try to reconstruct what actually happened and who moved the stone and so on on the basis of that, just hopeless, we simply haven't got enough evidence."

Well, so, first thing, why I'm not going to give my account of what happened in the Easter events is that my major point is that we simply have not got enough evidence to reconstruct what happened then. Second thing, there was much I agreed with in what Dr. Habermas said, including some of the things that he was offering as arguments against me, because I certainly wouldn't want to defend what Hume actually wrote. I did, I think, say that I thought that there were gross weaknesses in what Hume actually wrote. I was offering something that was a development of that.

Now, neither did I offer a contention about miracles as something unfalsifiable. Oh no, surely I made the point that if we were in a position to start where Cardinal Newman wanted to start, you know, if we knew that there was a God who was wanting to make an acceptable and intelligible and understood revelation, all these things, then indeed we might be able to do it, but if one is not starting from that, then one can't do it.

Then, about natural impossibility and laws of nature, well, I think I want to repeat my point that both sides in this debate have a vested interest in insisting on strong notions of natural necessity and natural impossibility, because only if you have a strong idea of a natural order can you suggest that this natural order, if it's overridden, is in this overriding evidence of a supernatural power at work. I'm certainly not dogmatically saying that miracles are inconceivable; on the contrary! I'm explaining that I understand a miracle to be an overriding by a supernatural power of the natural order. I know other physicists say this, but then other physicists say the opposite with equal assurance. They say, "Flew, you've got it all wrong. *All* physicists know . . ."

Then when I repeat what I've been told that all physicists know to the next physicist I meet, "You've got it *all* wrong, Flew, you're simply ignorant of physics. *All* physicists know the opposite." Well, the main point I want you to grasp is that all of us here have a vested interest in the idea of a strong natural order. This ought to be taken as agreed because it's only if there is that strong natural order that there is anything significant about the Resurrection.

Supposing Habermas came up to me and said, "You know, Flew, you're an absolute bigot, resurrections are happening every day of the week in Lynchburg. You ignorant, prejudiced Englishman, you come here saying this can't happen. We do it regularly!" Well, okay, if I came here and found it was happening left, right, and center, I would have to shake up my ideas, but one of the things that it would lead me to think would be, "Wow! Then it probably did happen in Jerusalem in A.D. 30—but so what! Nothing remarkable about Jesus' Resurrection, people in Lynchburg are doing it every day of the week." You really have got to make a miracle naturally impossible if it's going to be something the occurrence of which is exciting.

Then about these Pauline experiences. I think it is significant that Paul offers his own experience on the road to Damascus about which he never claims, you know, that he pressed his fingers in the wounds. He doesn't say this. No, Jesus makes all these appearances, but there's nothing out of the way about a vision when there isn't anything out there that it's a vision of, you know. No one would want to dispute that Bernadette (Marie-Bernarde Soubirous), around whose visions the whole cult of Lourdes arose, no one would want to dispute that she was an honest peasant girl who did indeed have the vision. What the dispute is about, is was this caused by the surviving Mother of God or was there anything there, you know, that the cameras, the television team, the people using instruments, and so on, would have weighed. Well, I take it that Paul is not even claiming that. He's claiming that it was one of these bodies that you put on when corruption puts on incorruption. Now, this is why I made the fuss about all the people concerned being believing Jews, and Paul in particular being a Pharisee believing in the Resurrection and so on. This is why that's significant.

He has an experience that is nothing miraculous in itself, and he then interprets it as he's seen not an ordinary flesh and blood body, but a spiritual Resurrection body.

Then, about some of the other things I was talking about. What I think is significant is that what I understood was agreed was that the earliest documents that we have don't have any of the references to the contents of our Gospels that you would expect someone who was preaching the Christian religion as it is now understood to include. Paul never refers to any of the supposedly dominical sayings in the Gospels, never refers to any of the birth stories, never refers to any of these other things. They come in at some later stage. On the road to Damascus (of course I'm not going to deny that Paul had the experience on the road to Damascus that changed his life, certainly this happened), what is in dispute is whether what he was confronted with was what was supposed to have left the tomb, a corruptible body of Jesus of Nazareth. I don't think he's even claiming this.

The point I made about Peter was not that there's not a Gospel record of an appearance to Peter, of course there is, it's the first appearance to Peter that is not even in Matthew. Everyone who knows the Roman church knows Matthew is the favorite Gospel of the church of Rome because of its general emphasis on Peter. Now this is a very odd thing. The writer of the Gospel, later on, who's wanting to build up the position of Peter doesn't say that the first appearance was to Peter, he doesn't seem to have heard about this at all. Isn't it also remarkable that this supposedly enormously sensational collective vision of more than one hundred people is absolutely unmentioned in the Gospels.

Then, about liars. What I hoped I was going to avoid was this sort of eighteenth-century discussion, trial of the witnesses, you've either got to say that these people who died for their convictions were deliberate, conscious liars who cooked the whole story up, you know, in a crafty afternoon. "What stories shall we tell the press?" It is, of course, ridiculous to suggest that, but there's an awful lot of room between recording what actually happened a long time ago and telling deliberate lies about what actually happened a long time ago.

Why I brought in this stuff about the birth stories was that I thought that this was an example both sufficiently close and sufficiently far away of the way in which the consideration of what was thought to be a prophecy was leading people to adapt their views about what actually happened, arguing, obviously with complete integrity, they thought they knew that in Isaiah this was a prophecy of the birth of the Messiah. They believed also that Jesus was the Messiah. I believe the word *christos* is the translation of the Hebrew for Messiah. So they took it they knew that if he was the Messiah and this was a prophecy, which both things were granted, he must have been born in Bethlehem. So the whole thing would seem to them is that we are trying to find what actually happened. We know, don't we, he must have been born in Bethlehem, so how do we account for his being born in Bethlehem? We then scratch around for someone telling a story that might explain the Bethlehem birth. Now, I think this again is significant, how people, utterly honest, utterly dedicated people can over a long time come up with an explanation. You've got people with a specific framework of ideas, specific assumptions, talking with one another, arguing about it, worrying about it, "How do we interpret the visions, you know, we've had these visions, how do we interpret them?" They would come to conclusions very far removed from whatever actually happened.

I want to end by saying I do not believe that anyone is in a position to know what actually happened there, and if ten thousand scholars tell me that they are all agreed that they know that Jesus' tomb was opened on such and such a day, I want to ask them, On what evidence do you know this? You know, when was it recorded and so on. Well, it was, in anyone's view, a long time after, with much going on in between. Well, this wouldn't matter if it wasn't of such ideological importance, because one would just assume that there's no reason for anyone to get this wrong. Again, the point I was making from the beginning is that the sort of evidence that you need for the establishment of a miraculous event is much stronger than the evidence you need for saying that your daughter went out and got a Coke yesterday afternoon. You need much better evidence, so these considerations are a serious matter.

Rebuttal: Gary R. Habermas

Let me address myself in order to a number of Dr. Flew's claims. I'm going to go back to his original paper and to one of his claims, which, as far as I'm aware, is the only major one on the subject of Jesus' Resurrection that I didn't already say something about in my initial paper. This is his statement that even if the Resurrection of Jesus occurred, there's still the matter of identification. How do we know that it was God who raised Jesus? I will simply outline what I think is a two-fold case for the identification of the Resurrection. How do we know that the Resurrection was an act of God? I will propose two sets of arguments and I will preface them by saying that these are inductive, not deductive.

First of all, what I call a prospective argument proceeds from God's existence forward to the Resurrection. We have agreed not to discuss God's existence or arguments for God's existence, but because Dr. Flew asked me the question, I will tell him the line I would take, without using any single argument. I would say first of all that there are good arguments for God's existence, and second of all that the Resurrection is an event that is consistent with God's attributes. Dr. Flew disagrees with me about God's existence, but I know he agrees that if God's existence could be shown to be true, the general line of my argument from God's existence to the Resurrection follows. For I quote Dr. Flew, "Certainly given some beliefs about God, the occurrence of the resurrection does become enormously more likely."[1] So the Resurrection as an act of God does follow from such a basis.

The second argument is one that I call retrospective, and it views Jesus, as we do today, in a post-Easter sense. How can one look back at the claims of Jesus? One does so through the Cross and Resurrection. One cannot see the claims of Jesus unless one looks through his Cross and Resurrection, as did most of the early Jewish believers of the first century. The Resurrection made a difference concerning the claims of

Christ. Jesus claimed to have a unique relationship with the God of the universe. This is recognized by virtually all critical scholars today. I'll just mention Rudolf Bultmann as an example of one who admits that Jesus believed this.[2]

There are at least four major indications that Jesus taught that he had a unique relationship with the God of the universe. First of all, this is shown by his self-designations. He claimed that he was the Son of Man and even that he was the Son of God. Let me refer you to Christologies such as those by Oscar Cullmann, Raymond Brown, and Wolfhart Pannenberg[3] for some of the various details. Jesus used terms such as *Abba,* which can be translated as either "Father" or even "Daddy" from the Aramaic, as an evidence of a claim to a unique relationship with God. Let me mention Jeremias on this point.[4]

Second, Jesus claimed authority, unlike any founder of any other major religion in the history of religions. For instance, other religious founders have said, in effect, "I'll show you the way of salvation." Jesus said, "I am the way of salvation." Other religious founders have said, "I'll lead you to the right path." Jesus said, "I am the right path." Again, this is admitted by Fuller, Bultmann,[5] and others. Jesus made unique claims concerning salvation. He also said he could forgive sin (Mark 2:1–12). And when the critics came up to him and said, "Well, you know only God can do that," the implication becomes obvious. Jesus was making a specific claim. Cullmann, for example, has made strong statements about this passage.[6]

Third, his actions showed that he could do more than just make claims. Jesus fulfilled Old Testament prophecy. (Concerning Dr. Flew's mention of the birth narratives in this context, let me just parenthetically add here that I think that they are irrelevant to the subject of the Resurrection. But I would still like to see Dr. Flew respond to A. N. Sherwin-White, an eminent Oxford University Roman historian who defended the Palestinian census that Dr. Flew called a "wildly implausible tale" earlier tonight.[7] And a number of scholars, such as F. F. Bruce, have also defended this account in Luke 2.[8])

But considering Old Testament prophecy, some interesting arguments have been published concerning Isaiah 53, for instance, written by Martin Hengel, Oscar Cullmann,[9] and others, where they argue that Jesus did believe he was fulfilling this prophecy. Now did the Jews believe that the Servant of Isaiah 53 was the Messiah? Well, some early Jewish commentaries do indicate that Jews often understood the Servant of Isaiah 53 to be the Messiah.[10]

Additionally, Jesus said that his miracles were a sign that what he said was true. Edwin Yamauchi, professor of ancient history at Miami University in Ohio, said that Jesus is the only founder of a major world religion for whom there is eyewitness testimony of his miracles.[11] Dr. Flew, Dr. Miethe, and I were in Dallas a few months ago for a number of debates between theists and atheists. On the New Testament panel, two scholars represented the skeptical alternative to the evangelical viewpoint. Even both these critics admitted that the evidence indicated that Jesus performed historical miracles.[12] Jesus said that such were further evidence of his claims.

And last, Jesus said that his Resurrection would be *the* sign that his claims were true. If he did rise, it would be the sign of his unique connection with God. Again, his actions indicate that he was correct.

A fourth indicator of Jesus' claims is the reactions of others toward him. According to Mark 14:61–62, one of the major instigations for Jesus' death was that when asked the question, "Are you the Messiah, the Son of God?" he replied, "I am." And Rudolf Bultmann, Reginald Fuller, Raymond Brown, and others all say that even his New Testament followers applied the title of God to Jesus.[13]

Now these are some of Jesus' claims. Anybody can make claims, but the facts show that this same Jesus also fulfilled prophecy and performed miracles; in particular, he was raised from the dead. And it is reasonable that Jesus would be best able to explain the purpose behind the Resurrection. To repeat, he made unique claims, and he was uniquely raised from the dead. Jesus' testimony is that as the chief miracle, the Resurrection was the major sign that his worldview was verified by an act of God. The only time that a resurrection can be shown to have literally taken place, it occurred to the only person who made such unique claims about his own deity, his special message, and other things concerning his relationship with God. The Resurrection is therefore not a "brute fact" of history that stands alone. Rather, the Resurrection, in conjunction with the claims of Jesus, shows that what Jesus taught is true.[14]

A couple other things that Dr. Flew expressed also need to be mentioned. He said that we need both strong laws of nature and strong exceptions to these laws. I agree, although I don't like the word *violate*. I would say that miracles temporarily supersede the laws of nature, that is, the normally observed and known pattern of nature. I don't think we can say that we know all about the laws of nature, so I think a miracle supersedes the normally observed and known pattern of nature. This point addresses the concern for strong laws, because it is agreed that an interruption occurs at the level of an empirical observation of these laws. And because I believe that miracles temporarily supersede such an observed pattern, I also hold to strong exceptions brought about by God in order to confirm a message, which is very close to David Hume's definition.[15] I would also respectfully ask Dr. Flew if he could produce a formula that would better account for the evidence for Jesus' Resurrection. In some of his works he suggests that if a miracle were shown to be true, we should expand the laws of nature. He and others make this suggestion. Now what are we going to say about the Resurrection? In order to expand the laws of nature you're going to have something like this: the only time there's an exception to the law of death is with this man called Jesus of Nazareth. I think that's a point in our favor.

There are several other brief points that Dr. Flew mentioned both in his initial paper and in his rebuttal that I want to refer to quickly. Dr. Flew said that it was odd that God would reveal himself only to the Jews. Wolfhart Pannenberg's popular thesis is that God revealed himself in the Resurrection to everyone through the medium of public history, not just to the Jews.[16] The very fact that an Englishman and an American can stand up here and debate this today shows that it is much more than a Jewish affair.

Dr. Flew questioned some of the data of the Gospels. Let me make three important points here. First, I based my core historical facts argument on the data that the vast majority of scholars accept, thereby making objections to other areas of scripture irrelevant at this point.

Second, the Gospels can be shown to be reliable sources anyway. Third, we have a lot more material about the historical Jesus than that in the New Testament alone. Dr. Flew was espousing, I believe, a thesis such as that of G. A. Wells when he questioned the amount of history in the Epistles.[17] Well, first of all, the purpose of the Epistles was not to present history. But second, let me just challenge him to respond to the fact that within 100 to 150 years after the birth of Christ, approximately eighteen non-Christian, extrabiblical sources from secular history, none of them Christian, mention more than one hundred facts, beliefs, and teachings from the life of Christ and early Christendom. These items, I might add, mention almost every major detail of Jesus' life, including miracles, the Resurrection, and his claims to be deity. Now, Dr. Flew might say that these are late sources. But these sources are much closer to the events that they describe than are key portions of historical material recorded by the ancient Roman historians Livy and Tacitus.

But let's handle another "late" claim. Dr. Flew keeps going back to this time of ten to twenty years after the Crucifixion for the earliest Christian writings. He also states that the earliest account is not ten to twenty years later, but that it's 1 Corinthians, some twenty years after. Now I think he's missed my point, and this is crucial. The pre-Pauline creed may have been written down for the first time in 1 Corinthians 15, but the creed was an oral confession that dates from a much earlier time. Many New Testament critical scholars today, such as Reginald Fuller, provide details on this creed.[18] It was transmitted orally to Paul, who recorded the creed after he received it, about three to eight years after the Crucifixion. Is this too long a time? No. Rather, it is an amazingly early report. But, as I said, one can get even two stages earlier than that. According to most scholars, Paul received this creed from the apostles, which makes it even earlier, and a creed has to be repeated before it becomes stylized. So now we're right on top of the Crucifixion, and note, it's the eyewitnesses who transmitted this information; it's not hearsay testimony.

According to major New Testament scholars, it was Peter and James who gave this message to the Apostle Paul. So although this confession is recorded in 1 Corinthians, the eyewitness testimony was noised abroad via witnesses from right after the Crucifixion itself. So far Dr.

Flew has not answered this evidence, which has changed the view, as I said, of perhaps most of the critical theologians of the present generation. Wolfhart Pannenberg has said on at least a couple occasions that most critical theologians today are willing to admit that the disciples really saw something that might be called visions of the risen Jesus.[19] The discussions take various forms, such as the nature of Jesus' spiritual body, but most scholars are willing to admit that the disciples saw visions of Jesus. Then Pannenberg goes on to say that hallucinations or other alternate naturalistic theories are not acceptable.[20]

Dr. Flew states that we can't tell what happened back then, that it's too obscure or cloudy. But that's exactly the purpose of my recitation of the core historical facts, exactly the purpose. Probably the reason he says we can't tell is because he doesn't have a naturalistic theory to propose. In other words, all the historical facts we do have, and that scholars agree on, support the literal Resurrection of Jesus.

Now I would like to talk further about the hallucination theory, which Dr. Flew hinted at twice. Perhaps in our head-to-head discussion he will tell me about the hallucination theory. He also said, however, that he wouldn't give me a naturalistic theory. I think the reason he says we can't know what happened is because he doesn't have a concrete theory to propose. Again, he's got to come to grips with the case of the early eyewitness testimony given right after the Crucifixion by the men who said they saw the risen Jesus. Now if one doesn't believe they saw him, we're going to have to come up with some other explanation.

Further, Dr. Flew said that this case isn't even good enough for psychic research. Well, as far as I know, the research on the Shroud of Turin was more thorough than any research done on any single event in psychic studies. The shroud may not have warranted a mention in the psychic research annals, but it warranted probably the most intense investigation of any archaeological artifact in modern history.

Dr. Flew agreed in his initial paper that Hume is wrong in his essay on miracles, but he wants to update Hume. That, however, was just my point. I pointed out that Hume, even as updated by Dr. Flew, is mistaken and for practically the same reasons. I don't think he's answered my five objections to this updated Humean position.

One more point about G. A. Wells. Dr. Flew came from the

University of Michigan not too long ago. Dr. Wells was there and he presented his radical thesis that maybe Jesus never existed. Virtually nobody holds this position today. It was reported that Dr. Morton Smith of Columbia University, even though he is a skeptic himself, responded that Dr. Wells's view was "absurd."[21]

Let me say in closing that I've been attempting to get Dr. Flew to deal directly with the evidence for Jesus' Resurrection. I don't think he has done so. All he's said so far is that we can't tell what happened. Please notice, he's not dealt with the four kinds of evidence I've presented. I believe he has generally sidestepped them, yet in one of his essays on miracles, he admits my point when he asserts that "Our only way of determining the capacities and incapacities of nature is to study what does in fact occur."[22] I agree with you, Dr. Flew; we need to look at nature and see what does in fact occur. I've given you four sets of arguments for the Resurrection, and you haven't addressed yourself to the evidence. You say, "We don't need to, we can't get back to the original testimony." But we can.

Even after admitting that we need to study the original event, Dr. Flew further laments in this same essay that "To come closely to grips with the evidence available in particular cases would unfortunately carry us well beyond the limits of both length and subject specified in the present series."[23] In other words, "We need to look at the events, but I'm sorry, I don't have time here. We need to look at the facts that happen in nature, but I can't do it in this essay." But as far as I'm aware (although I may be wrong), he has not dealt with the evidence for the Resurrection in any of his published material on miracles. So my point is that he says we need to look at it, and then I don't think that he ever does.

In one work, however, he does take at least a brief look at the Resurrection. He mentions M. C. Perry's book, *The Easter Enigma,* and his reaction is interesting. I was surprised when Dr. Flew treated this book by M. C. Perry in a positive way, terming some of Perry's ideas "methodologically sound." And later he compliments Perry on his reasonableness.[24] The reason for my surprise at these compliments is that Perry advocates an actual Resurrection of Jesus' glorified body and he supports the notion of life after death. Dr. Flew says that Perry's theory is not actually miraculous, but the prototype for Perry's model, developed in the late nineteenth century by Theodor Keim, was admittedly miraculous.[25] But regardless of the miraculous element, we must note here that Dr. Flew has given some praise to a book that declares that Jesus actually was raised, spiritually and literally, and that life after death is a reality. Although my view differs from Perry's, it would appear that complimenting a theory of Jesus' literal though spiritual Resurrection would be a major point for my thesis tonight.

NOTES

1. Antony G. N. Flew, personal correspondence with Terry L. Miethe, April 1, 1985.
2. Rudolf Bultmann, *Theology of the New Testament,* vol. 1, trans. Kendrick Grobel (New York: Scribner, 1951, 1955) especially 7–9.
3. Oscar Cullmann, *The Christology of the New Testament,* trans. Shirley C. Guthrie and Charles A. M. Hall (Philadelphia: Westminster Press, 1963); Raymond Brown, *Jesus —God and Man* (Milwaukee: Bruce, 1967); Wolfhart Pannenberg, *Jesus—God and Man,* trans. Lewis L. Wilkins and Duane A. Priebe (Philadelphia: Westminster Press, 1968).
4. Joachim Jeremias, *The Central Message of the New Testament* (Philadelphia: Fortress Press, 1965), 9–30.
5. Reginald H. Fuller, *The Foundations of the New Testament Christology* (New York: Scribner, 1965), 105–106; Bultmann, *Theology of the New Testament,* vol. 1, 7–9.
6. Cullmann, *Christology of the New Testament,* 282.
7. A. N. Sherwin-White, *Roman Society and Roman Law in the New Testament* (London: Oxford University Press, 1963; Grand Rapids, MI: Baker Book House, 1978), 162–171.
8. F. F. Bruce, *Jesus and Christian Origins Outside the New Testament* (Grand Rapids, MI: Eerdmans, 1974), 192–194.
9. Martin Hengel, *The Atonement,* trans. John Bowden (Philadelphia: Fortress Press, 1981); Cullmann, *Christology of the New Testament,* 282.
10. Frederick Aston, *The Challenge of the Ages,* sixteenth ed., rev., published by the author in Scarsdale, NY in 1962 and containing a preface by Robert H. Pfeiffer.
11. Edwin Yamauchi, *Jesus, Zoroaster, Socrates, Buddha, Muhammed* (Downers Grove, IL: Inter Varsity Press, 1974), 40.
12. In a debate entitled "The Historical Foundations of Christianity," Howard Kee and Robert M. Price argued for the skeptical position against conservatives Earl Ellis and R. T. France. The dialogue took place at the Dallas Hilton, Dallas, TX, on February 9, 1985.
13. Cf. Bultmann, *Theology of the New Testament,* 129; Fuller, *Foundations of New Testament Christology,* 208, 248–249, for instances; Brown, *Jesus—God and Man,* "Does the New Testament Call Jesus God?"
14. See Gary R. Habermas, *The Resurrection of Jesus: An Apologetic* (Grand Rapids, MI: Baker Book House, 1980), "The Existence of God" and "The Person and Teachings of Christ."

15. Hume, *An Enquiry Concerning Human Understanding*, section 10, "Of Miracles," Part 1.

16. See especially Wolfhart Pannenberg, ed., *Revelation as History*, trans. David Granskou (New York: Macmillan, 1968).

17. G. A. Wells, *Did Jesus Exist?* (Buffalo: Prometheus Books, 1975).

18. Fuller, *The Foundation of the Resurrection Narratives* (New York: Macmillan, 1971), "The Earliest Easter Traditions."

19. For example, Wolfhart Pannenberg, "A Dialogue on Christ's Resurrection," *Christianity Today* 12 (April 12, 1968): 5–12.

20. Pannenberg, *Jesus—God and Man*, 88–106.

21. Kate DeSmet, "Biblical Accounts of Jesus' Divinity Debated by Scholars," *Detroit News*, April 20, 1985, sec. A, Religion page.

22. Antony Flew, "The Credentials of Revelation: Miracle and History," in his *God and Philosophy* (New York: Dell, 1966), 149.

23. *Ibid.*, 154.

24. *Ibid.*, 155–156.

25. For details of Keim's view, published in 1872, see W. J. Sparrow-Simpson, *The Resurrection and the Christian Faith* (1911; reprint, Grand Rapids, MI: Zondervan, 1968), 110–120. Cf. Albert Schweitzer, *The Quest of the Historical Jesus*, trans. by W. Montgomery (New York: Macmillan) 210–214.

Head-to-Head:
Habermas—Flew

HABERMAS: I think we're supposed to fight it out.

FLEW: I'll start then. About the Resurrection and the whole story becoming more probable with the belief in God, and not just a belief that the universe had a beginning by, was produced by, some sort of power. Surely, to make any account of the supposed Easter events more probable, you've got to have a much richer notion of God than as just a Creator, you've got to have some of the elements that I gave in that quotation from Cardinal Newman. You've got to have some reason for believing he's going to want to produce an intelligible revelation, and presumably Newman was taking for granted the Old Testament story of the chosen people and the Messiah, and therefore thinking that he was in the position, in thinking of this matter, of a Jew contemporary with Jesus who was wondering whether Jesus was the Messiah.

HABERMAS: I have no problem there, and, as I said, I don't want to pursue evidence for God. But I agree with you. Something more substantial than a mere belief in God's existence has to be there, but I would say that we can argue for coherence with regards to the Resurrection. Let's introduce a hypothetical situation here. A naturalist is arguing with a theist about the Resurrection, and the theist pushes the naturalist and the naturalist comes to admit that, indeed, the Resurrection is a historical event. At that point, would the naturalist have to be at least open to the theist's claims that Jesus is deity and that he speaks authoritatively from God?

FLEW: Yes, that seems to be clear.

HABERMAS: So this is a legitimate argument and the naturalist would have to be open to Jesus' claims?

FLEW: I don't know what he's going to do next. But yes, you've put it rather nicely. You'd have to be open to it. What would happen next, I don't know. But clearly there would have to be some ears opened to some radical new thinking.

HABERMAS: You mean new thinking on the part of the naturalist.

FLEW: Yes, but where the radical new thinking would go, heaven knows.

HABERMAS: Dr. Flew, twice you made quick references to hallucinations.

FLEW: Yes.

HABERMAS: So you might say that the disciples (or Paul) saw something that was not objectively present. The hallucination theory was popular about one hundred years ago, and it was ruled out later. It suffered from a number of shortcomings. In the Miracles class that I teach, which is substantially on the Resurrection, I produce twenty-two refutations of the hallucination theory. Now these are of varying importance and strength. But one point I want to make is that hallucinations are private events observed by one person alone. Two people cannot see the same hallucination, let alone eleven. If eleven people saw Jesus on one occasion, few contemporary scholars would argue that it was a hallucination. That theory has been thoroughly critiqued.

Let me say a couple other things concerning the various circumstances of the Resurrection appearances of Jesus. There are too many different times, places, and people involved for the hallucination theory to be valid, and psychological preconditions are lacking. If I can quote from a clinical psychologist here, I'll see if you still want to push the hallucination theory. Let me quote from a well-published psychologist, who says,

Hallucinations are individual occurrences. By their very nature only one person can see a given hallucination at a time. They certainly are not something which can be seen by a group of people. Neither is it possible that one person could somehow induce an hallucination in somebody else. Since an hallucination exists only in this subjective, personal sense, it is obvious that others cannot witness it.[1]

And this scholar concludes by saying, "For anyone to prove [that the disciples saw hallucinations of the risen Jesus] they would have to go against much of the current psychiatric and psychological data about the nature of hallucinations."[2] Now because you proposed the hallucination theory, let me remind you that you did the same in Dallas when we met three months ago. I replied then that two people couldn't see the same hallucination. You responded that I was correct and that was the end of that discussion. I wonder why you brought it back up again tonight and if you want to pursue it?

FLEW: I was only offering this suggestion in the case of Paul, which is the appearance story for which we have the best evidence, which is the statement of the subject himself made not long after the conversion experience in question. It seems to me that Paul is not claiming that he was actually seeing something that would have been visible to anyone else that happened to be there. He was claiming that he had a vision of Jesus with his spiritual body. And I take it that an incorruptible, spiritual body would not normally be visible. He doesn't say it was visible to other people, does he?

HABERMAS: I don't know how you can argue . . .

FLEW: Because if it were visible to other people, there would have been more than one person who saw the appearance on the road to Damascus.

HABERMAS: I don't know how you can ignore the other events surrounding Jesus' appearance to Paul, when the texts provide additional details. And in those instances, although we don't know exactly what his companions saw, we are told that they did see the light and did hear some sounds, although they were not able to comprehend the message. But you also said that Paul's account is early, so he offers the best evidence. But the creed reports the testimony of the disciples before Paul's experience even occurred. So if you're going to grant me early evidence for Paul's appearance, what do we say about the disciples?

FLEW: Of course, of course, the claim, the crucial claim that Jesus was resurrected was part of the doctrine of Christian communities presumably before Paul wrote to one of them in 1 Corinthians. That's not in dispute. What is in dispute is whether this creed contains stories of the Resurrection appearances. Because modern creeds certainly don't contain more than He rose on the third day, and so on.

HABERMAS: Starting with verse 5 of 1 Corinthians 15, we have a number of appearances recorded in the creed, and Cephas (Peter) starts the list off. And I think that most New Testament scholars who have pursued the subject have concluded that Paul received this list from Peter and James in Jerusalem on his first visit to the city. By the way, there's an alternative theory, which says he received the creed in Damascus. That would place it even earlier than the Jerusalem date.

FLEW: Yes, but he got this story about the appearances to other people and then he rather oddly discovered that this appearance to him on the road to Damascus was the last one. He got the story, but that isn't the same thing as getting the creed. Now I'm not disputing that there was some sort of creed that all the first members of the Christian churches adhered to, but if it was anything like the Nicene Creed, say, it wouldn't have contained evidence for the Resurrection in the shape of so-and-so and so-and-so saw the resurrected Jesus. If something like this was kicking around, it would have been in something else other than the creed.

HABERMAS: But this early creed *did* report eyewitness appearances to the risen Jesus. Starting with verse 5, it mentions Peter and goes through a half-dozen appearances, ending with Paul. At least some appearances are included in the creed. So let me ask you, do you believe that the original disciples saw hallucinations? You have said you were referring only to Paul.

FLEW: Ah, well, what I don't believe is that there were collective hallucinations where the twelve saw it all at once.

HABERMAS: So you don't believe that the disciples saw collective hallucinations.

FLEW: I don't believe that there was anyone necessarily at the time who claimed that. You know, you keep talking about the whole situation as if the Gospels contained material that the authors were supposed to be telling you now and you were in Jerusalem at the time, you were hearing from these chaps in Jerusalem at the time, and you know it happened down there. And then you say that, oh well, they're saying that Jesus said this, and you take it that Jesus said the things that years afterward they said he said in Jerusalem at the time.

HABERMAS: But I'm not talking about a period of years afterward. I'm only talking about the Resurrection appearances that the disciples reported and handed down to Paul. I also mentioned that Luke 24:34 records an appearance to Peter, a report that is as early as the Pauline creed.[3] Now if Paul got his creed from the eyewitnesses, and the eyewitnesses claim to have seen Jesus, yet you don't believe that the disciples saw hallucinations, then what did happen? What naturalistic theory accounts for the disciples' experiences?

FLEW: Here we have the earliest written document about appearances, and two things in it are inconsistent with what appears in the Gospels. Why didn't the writers of the Gospels report the appearance to the five hundred? Supposing you wanted to tell me about the appearance to five hundred as a thing that couldn't be accounted for by a collective hallucination. Now, wouldn't the Gospel writers, if they were familiar with this story and believed it was true, have brought this into the Gospels?

HABERMAS: The Gospel of Matthew does say that Jesus appeared on a hillside. More may have been there than just the eleven disciples. Besides, I never mentioned the five hundred. I don't think I brought them up once. I still want to base the case on the eleven disciples, who claimed they saw the risen Jesus. Let me paraphrase Rudolf Bultmann who, in his influential 1941 essay "New Testament and Mythology," said that history can prove that the earliest disciples believed that they saw the risen Jesus.[4]

FLEW: Ah.

HABERMAS: Now, what do we do if these were not hallucinations? What were they?

FLEW: They believed they saw him. Now, this is a very different thing from saying that they claimed as a group, "I say, we've all seen the risen Jesus, all of us together." What we've got is the claim that they had all seen him. That's not the claim they'd all seen him on the same occasion.

HABERMAS: But the group appearance to the disciples is recorded in the creed. 1 Corinthians 15:5 says that Jesus first appeared to Peter, then to the twelve disciples. I repeat, Jesus appeared to the twelve. That's the second appearance recorded, and it provides just what you are asking. Now, you have already granted to me that this is an early report and you've already granted that Paul is a good source, but this is even earlier for the other eyewitnesses. And it does say that he appeared to the twelve. This list also includes an appearance "to all of the apostles" (1 Cor. 15:7). So we have two separate appearances, to the twelve and to the apostles. So that's in the creed, it's eyewitness testimony, and it dates back to the time of the Crucifixion.

FLEW: Wait a minute, eyewitness testimony. There's a statement in Paul that there was a collective appearance to the twelve apostles, but we haven't got the testimony directly of even one of the twelve. What we have is a statement from Paul that this happened to those twelve other people, and that is very different.

HABERMAS: Let me respond to that in two ways. First of all, Paul received the list from Peter and James, according to the majority of testimony today in New Testament scholarship. He received it from them, so at least Peter is saying that he and the other ten disciples collectively saw the risen Jesus. I additionally made the point in my initial essay that in 1 Corinthians 15:11, 14, and 15, Paul states that the message that he was proclaiming was the same as that proclaimed by the apostles. So Paul states that the disciples and he were preaching the same thing about the resurrected Jesus. Paul is not relating circumstantial material; in fact, the creed is not his material at all, as Paul clearly states in verse 3. The creed is an eyewitness report given to Paul, in all likelihood, by persons who saw Jesus.

Second, although many critical scholars today would not grant that the Gospels were written by eyewitnesses such as the disciples, many scholars find a large amount of eyewitness testimony behind the Gospels. For example, Raymond Brown, in writing a major commentary on perhaps the most disputed of the four Gospels, John, concludes that the Apostle John is the chief contributor to the historical tradition behind the Gospel.[5] In the Gospel of John we have two chapters giving evidence concerning the appearances of the risen Jesus. I also mentioned in my opening essay that C. H. Dodd, in an interesting essay on form critical studies, concluded that there are a number of early testimonies in the Gospel accounts of the Resurrection. So when you say we don't have any eyewitness testimony in the Gospels you're going to have to argue with eminent scholars such as Raymond Brown and C. H. Dodd. And concerning the creed, many scholars who are not in my camp say that the earliest eyewitnesses reported the Resurrection appearances of Jesus. In fact, in a famous debate between Bultmann and Barth, Barth said that we ought not to ask for evidence for the Resurrection; we should believe on faith alone. But Bultmann replied that although he agreed with Barth that we don't need evidence for faith (they're both Kierkegaardians), it's clear that Paul was attempting to give evidence for Jesus' Resurrection by citing the list of appearances in 1 Corinthians 15:5–7. You can check that in volume I of *Theology of the New Testament* by Rudolf Bultmann.[6] Again, I'm citing people who don't always agree with me, but who say that my thesis is sound as far as the original disciples reporting that they saw appearances of the risen Jesus. You've already told me that you don't think that this testimony is accounted for by collective hallucinations, but that we don't have the testimony of the disciples that they saw Jesus collectively. But we do have such testimony. They gave the creed to Paul, and then Paul added that the apostles preached the same Resurrection that he did. And we additionally have eyewitness testimony, including just such group appearances reported in the Gospels.

FLEW: Yes, there's plenty of room in this period, slips on what are fairly small things. The difference between claiming that several people had visions of the risen Jesus and claiming that they all simultaneously had the same one is the sort of difference that we agree is important. It is not clear that the people at the time would have seen this as important, is it?

HABERMAS: It appears to me that I have already clearly answered your question. You said a while ago that we don't have the disciples' testimony about the appearances. I pointed out that we did. You then said that the creed didn't report any collective experiences, and I responded that the creed reports the appearance to the twelve. And you're still saying that we don't know if the visions were simultaneous. Well, the creed states that Jesus appeared to the twelve and to all of the apostles. This is an eyewitness report of appearances of the risen Jesus to the twelve simultaneously.

FLEW: I mean I don't think we have the testimony of the disciples. What we have is Paul saying that two of the disciples told him something about them and the others. This is very different from having an account from the people themselves.

HABERMAS: Well, no, the evidence shows that Paul got it from the eyewitnesses themselves. And I don't think that virtually any scholars doubt that I Corinthians is the work of Paul. Paul took great care to interview the apostles personally in order to ascertain the nature of the Gospel, which includes the Resurrection (Gal. 1:18–20; 2:1–10). It is quite unlikely that Paul was completely wrong in this reported creed, especially since he so carefully checked out its content and indicated that the Resurrection was the central truth of the Christian faith. So even if Paul simply recorded the testimony of eyewitnesses, most likely Peter and James, then we've still got some strong and early eyewitness testimony. But as I said in my initial paper, this creedal material is not Paul's. It is an early eyewitness report, which is what you are requesting.

FLEW: He takes it that they had visions.

HABERMAS: No, they told him that they saw the risen Jesus.

FLEW: They told him that they saw the risen Jesus.

HABERMAS: Yes. "They" are the eyewitnesses. And second, we have some eyewitness testimony from the Gospels.

FLEW: But what is to be understood in Paul, presumably, is that they had the same sort of experience as he is claiming to have had. You see, he makes this claim, which doesn't involve physical contact. This is a claim that we'll refer to Shakespeare's Macbeth, "Is this a dagger which I see before me, its handle toward mine hand?" And then there is a test as to whether it's a hallucinatory experience or an actual dagger. "Come, let me clutch thee." Now Paul is taking it that it's an important vision in the way it's caused, but that his experience was like that. I think what is significant is that Paul puts his own experience, which is definitely not the sort of claim that's made about doubting Thomas, in the group of the others. Now you want to construe the others as being in the doubting Thomas category and leave Paul's, which he regards as being the same as all the others.

HABERMAS: You'd have to show me that Paul claimed that his appearance was of the same nature as that of the disciples. I don't think Paul said that. Paul said that his appearance came later.

FLEW: Yes, one born out of due time.

HABERMAS: Right, one born out of due time. He said the appearance to him was not at the same time as the appearance to them. He used the Greek word *horaō*. It was an old critical habit to say that the word *horaō* was utilized for "spiritual vision," and therefore Paul had said that the appearances to the disciples were the same as the appearance to him. Today that argument is not repeated as often, because the word *horaō* means not only "bodily appearance" more frequently than it does "spiritual appearance" in the New Testament, but second, *horaō* is the same Greek word that Luke uses when in his account Jesus tells the disciples to touch him because he is not a ghost (Luke 24:39). So you have to prove that Paul is saying that Jesus appeared to him in the same manner that he appeared to the disciples. I don't see that anywhere in Paul. I think Paul was arguing that Jesus literally appeared to him, period. I don't think Paul answers the question of whether he could touch Jesus or whether he saw him eat. Paul just ignores those issues.

FLEW: This is all in the context of those puzzling paragraphs about corruption putting on incorruption and how wrong it is to take the Resurrection body as being an ordinary body. Now it doesn't seem to me that someone who is going to say all that would say all that without also saying that what he saw was not like this but something substantially different from this. He's going to say all these things about corruption and incorruption.

HABERMAS: But the Gospel testimony is not that Jesus came back in the same corruptible body with the same limitations. As I mentioned briefly in my initial paper, the Gospels and Paul agree on an important fact: the resurrected Jesus had a new spiritual body. The Gospels never present Jesus walking out of the tomb. The Resurrection, per se, is never recorded in the Gospels, only the Resurrection appearances. When the stone is rolled away, Jesus does not walk out the way he does in the apocryphal literature. He's already gone, so he presumably exited through rock. Later he appears in buildings and then he disappears at will. The Gospels are clearly saying that Jesus was raised in a spiritual body. It was his real body, but it was changed, including new, spiritual qualities. And again, Paul uses the word *horaō,* the same Greek word used by Luke. I was referring earlier to a book by A. N. Sherwin-White, published by Oxford University Press, and Dr. Flew told me during the break that he studied under Sherwin-White.

FLEW: My old Ancient History tutor, yes.

HABERMAS: Well, Sherwin-White asserts that the Book of Acts is virtually unquestioned by Roman historians, even in its details. He points out that its historicity has been confirmed.[7] And Acts is the same book that records the Resurrection appearance to Paul. And the appearances to the disciples begin volume two of the Gospel of Luke. But Luke has no problem recording both the bodily appearances of Jesus and the appearance to Paul. Luke, the companion of Paul (as indicated by such signs as the "we" passages from Acts) relates the appearances to the disciples in the Gospel and Acts 1 as well as Paul's appearance in Acts. But I don't think you're going to be able to report many details about the Resurrection appearance to Paul unless you use the Book of Acts. And the Book of Acts was written by the man who wrote Luke, who had no problem teaching both the seemingly more substantial appearances of Jesus in the Gospels and the appearance to Paul on the road to Damascus. And we have reason to think that Acts is a good historical text.

FLEW: Yes, but anyone who believes that their visionary experience has been caused in a special way is, of course, going to use the word *see* without quotes around it. But that's not going to mean that the actual experience as described by someone who does not share that person's causal interpretation will be different from the experience of the person seeing it. Think of the Bernadette case, you see, where all the dispute within the Catholic church came after, I think, a bad start in which they wrongly questioned the honesty of Bernadette herself. All the dispute was not about the internal nature of the experience, but whether it had been spiritually caused; and I take it that no one was wanting to suggest that if the television cameras had been hiding behind, they would have gotten a picture of anything other than Bernadette.

HABERMAS: Virtually all scholars recognize that the eyewitnesses claimed to have literally seen the risen Jesus—not that they were expressing some spiritual conviction. And you brought up Bernadette again, but I don't think there's any comparison between that case and Jesus' Resurrection. I think the historical evidence for the Resurrection is much more substantial, but let me give you an example.

FLEW: But we've got Bernadette! We had the girl going back telling the village that right after the experience, for heaven's sake. We don't have someone some years later saying "Bernadette told me. . . ."

HABERMAS: Neither was the disciples' report years later. And we do have eyewitness reports of the risen Jesus. But unlike the Bernadette case, the disciples died for their message, and no naturalistic theories have explained away their report. At other points the evidence for Jesus' Resurrection is also stronger, such as the fact that the appearances to the disciples were collective.

NOTES

1. Gary R. Collins, personal correspondence with myself, February 21, 1977.
2. *Ibid.* Cf. J. P. Brady, "The Veridicality of Hypnotic, Visual Hallucinations," in Wolfram Keup, *Origin and Mechanisms of Hallucinations* (New York: Plenum Press, 1970), 181; Weston La Barre, "Anthropological Perspectives on Hallucination and Hallucinogens," in *Hallucinations: Behavior, Experience and Theory,* ed. R. K. Siegel and L. J. West (New York: John Wiley and Sons, 1975), 9–10.
3. See the reports of Jeremias, Bultmann, and Brown in footnote number 45 that follows my debate presentation.
4. Rudolf Bultmann, "New Testament and Mythology," revised translation by Reginald H. Fuller, in *Kerygma and Myth,* edited by Hans Werner Baitsch (New York: Harper & Row, 1961), 42.
5. Raymond E. Brown, *The Gospel According to John,* vol. 1 (Garden City, NY: Doubleday, 1966), 87–104.
6. Rudolf Bultmann, *Theology of the New Testament,* vol. 1, trans. Kendrick Grobel (New York: Scribner, 1951, 1955), 295.
7. Sherwin-White, *Roman Society and Roman Law in the New Testament* (Oxford: Oxford University Press, 1963; Grand Rapids, MI: Baker Book House, 1978), 189.

Question and Answer Period

TERRY L. MIETHE: Dr. Flew, if we cannot reconstruct the Easter events, do you at least have some account for the origin of the Easter story? How did it come about and why should the disciples have wanted to make Jesus the Old Testament Messiah by making these implausible claims?

FLEW: If I had to guess, I would suggest it arose out of something like the Pauline visions on the road to Damascus. But I am hesitant about this sort of thing; to speculate as to how people's religious beliefs arise is a dangerous thing to do. I mean, I wouldn't like to venture to offer an explanation as to how the Buddha succeeded in persuading people to become Buddhists without knowing a lot more about India and the time of the Buddha, for instance.

MIETHE: I was trying to get to the origin. Is there a naturalistic theory that would pinpoint it and say, "Okay, it was not a miraculous event, this is what really happened."

FLEW: I doubt it. I would contend that there are an enormous lot of things that we simply haven't got the evidence to know about. And I'll go back to this thing—if, even though considerably short of being omniscient and omnipotent, I wanted to make a revelation to all the peoples of the world, I think I could ensure that it got through to everyone, but then, of course, the response to that is that God's purposes are not known to us and he wasn't perhaps keen on its getting through to everyone or at least to everyone immediately. But you're only entitled to assume that it's possible to know this, I think, if you already believe a whole lot about God's intentions and that he wanted to make a revelation. If you already believe that this is his revelation, then I suppose you can reasonably presume that he's left enough available evidence for people, if they work hard enough, to discover what the message was he was wanting to convey. But unless you already have the assumptions about the divine intentions in the matter, I don't think you're entitled to conclude that there must be enough evidence to find out what actually happened at Easter, year unknown, but roughly in the early A.D. 30s.

MIETHE: Dr. Habermas, do you want to respond?

HABERMAS: Let me say three things, very briefly. Number one, I would just like to point out again that Dr. Flew has admitted that he's not going to give a naturalistic theory. I think that fact is substantial. Second, he said again that he thinks the nature of the disciples' experiences were like Paul's on the road to Damascus. I think we explored that in detail and people can decide for themselves what the evidence states.

But I want to say a third thing that I think is crucially important. I mentioned in my initial paper that a large group of critical theologians today, perhaps even a majority of the German theologians and especially the British thinkers, believe that Jesus was raised from the dead. I think that it is perhaps a majority view that the appearances to the disciples and to Paul consisted of a spiritual body. But this is the point. Where these scholars such as Wolfhart Pannenberg would disagree strongly, I think, with Dr. Flew, is that they would argue that even a more "spiritual" Resurrection does not rule out literal appearances of Jesus. They would argue that because there are no plausible naturalistic theories and because we can go back to the early creed and other such evidences, we therefore do have the early testimony of the disciples and even if it's a more spiritual Resurrection, Jesus was still actually raised from the dead. Now that's the position of these scholars, and I think that a large portion of them would say that even if it is true that the disciples' experiences were like Paul's, the disciples *still* witnessed literal appearances of Jesus. This is a key point, because these scholars will often argue for the literal, historical Resurrection based on appearances of a spiritual body. Again, I refer to Perry's book, which Dr. Flew himself referred to in one of his essays, where he complimented Perry. But Perry holds that Jesus really rose from the dead, although the appearances were more spiritual in nature. So the Resurrection of Jesus still follows from the line of argument Dr. Flew is pursuing.

W. DAVID BECK: Dr. Flew, Dr. Habermas has accused you of rejecting the existence of miracles a priori and if you wish to respond to that you may, but my real question is, What would have to take place in order to convince you that the existence of miracles is indeed possible?

FLEW: To persuade me that they are naturally possible, nothing would do that, because this idea is self-contradictory. To persuade me that they are possible by supernatural intervention is something that would be possible. From the beginning I have made it clear that I was not trying to rule out the occurrence of miracles a priori or by definition. On the contrary. I was saying that critical historians must start by assessing available evidence on the basis of what they know about what's probable or improbable, possible or impossible. They therefore must start by simply dismissing miracles stories out of hand. And all of us will do that in some cases. I doubt if there are many people here who believe St. Augustine's tale about two resurrections in his diocese in his lifetime, and certainly you won't believe miracles stories from Islam or Hinduism or any other non-Christian religion. So we're all in agreement about that. I then went on to say, yes, if someone wants to say, "We've got to shake up our normal assumptions, think afresh about a new case," they've got to produce some reason, and this reason could be either some sort of argument for an antecedent of miracles in a particular context; or a rich natural theology; or something about the evidence in a particular case. So what I am most emphatically not doing is dismissing it a priori or saying that it could not on any assumptions be proven to have happened. On the contrary, I think it could be. But I don't think it has been.

HABERMAS: I agree with Dr. Flew's first statement that a miracle such as a resurrection being caused by nature is impossible by definition. Unless God or some supernatural agent acts, there is no miracle, again by definition. So I am partially in sympathy with what David Hume says on this subject, as indicated by the fact that many of us argue against some miracle-claims at some times. But I will also say that I'm not opposed a priori to certain occasions of miracles occurring in other religions. I think there can be some reasons for that. But, Dr. Flew, let me ask you, are you saying that the spiritual Resurrection, a supernatural resurrection of Jesus, is possible? You said a natural one is not.

FLEW: Spiritual resurrection, you know, I should want to prove what's involved in this. I mean, spiritual bodies, it sounds like a body but with an adjective saying it's not. I suspect that a spiritual body is rather like an incorporeal body or an unmarried husband. This is a term that looks like a qualifying adjective, but isn't it a neutralizing one? How does a spiritual body differ from an imaginary or nonexistent body?

HABERMAS: So is a supernatural resurrection not possible, or is it possible?

FLEW: There are two questions here: one is about whether a resurrection is naturally possible. I take it it's naturally impossible, but no doubt this would be a small matter to omnipotence. Okay, so, it's, if you like, supernaturally possible and naturally impossible. Then about the spiritual body business. If the resurrection is a spiritual resurrection, I want to know how a spiritual body differs from a nonexistent one. What is the positive, discernible characteristic of a spiritual body that makes it a body as opposed to a vacuum?

HABERMAS: But you did say that a supernatural resurrection in a spiritual body is possible. You just said that, right?

FLEW: I haven't said anything about what's possible with a spiritual body, because I don't know what a spiritual body is. So before I answer any questions about the possibilities and impossibilities with spiritual bodies, I want to know what it is I'm supposed to say is possible or impossible.

HABERMAS: Earlier in discussing the Gospels I attempted to point out the most basic characteristics of a spiritual body. But is a literal, supernatural resurrection of Jesus possible?

FLEW: But, is a supernatural resurrection something that necessarily involves a spiritual body? In which case, I want to hear about a spiritual body. What I'm allowing to be supernaturally possible is you have someone who is dead as dead can be, cut up into pieces, if you like, to make it absolutely beyond all question that this person is 100 percent dead. Now I can understand the description of the pieces fitting together again and the dead person perks up, okay. Here you have a physical resurrection. Now because this is a describable phenomenon it is a conceivable occurrence, and I take it that if it occurred it could only be brought about by some exercise of supernatural power.

HABERMAS: I'm glad to hear your position is that a supernatural resurrection is at least possible.

MIETHE: Dr. Habermas, could you please give more details concerning the secular sources that mention the life and Resurrection of Jesus, and Dr. Flew, will you please respond?

HABERMAS: Yes, I think I made the comment in my rebuttal that there are approximately eighteen non-Christian writers who record more than one hundred events from the life, death, Resurrection of Jesus, and the beliefs of the earliest Christians. Now I suspect that Dr. Flew would say that they're comparatively late, because they are much later than the earliest creeds, and that's one major reason why I prefer to use the core facts and the early creed in 1 Corinthians 15. But we also need to remember that these secular sources are closer to the events that they report than are many ancient historians whose reports of events are well accepted as facts.

FLEW: Well, what are these facts? Do they include, for instance, the statements in Tacitus and in Pliny about the Christian church? Because there's absolutely nothing remarkable about a lot of statements from non-Christian sources about the activities of the Christian church and about what Christians believed about Jesus and about anything else. What would be remarkable would be if you suddenly found a lot of non-Christian sources saying, "And my goodness, we've just discovered that there was a resurrection and Pontius Pilate was procurator in

Judea." I take it that it's not that sort of statement about the life of Jesus for which you're saying there are a lot of non-Christian sources. But this is of no great evidential importance except, of course, for the study of the growth of the Christian church, and it's very important that there are non-Christian sources, fairly early on, for the development of the Christian church. That's for sure!

BECK: Dr. Habermas, Dr. Flew has said that because the accounts concerning the Resurrection were written ten to twenty years after they occurred, they never have been credible. Would you please comment on this proposed problem of textual inaccuracy?

HABERMAS: I'm not sure he said that the texts were inaccurate, he just said that they were ten to twenty years afterward.

FLEW: No, in fact, the textual authority, the earliness and the number of manuscripts for most of the Christian documents, is unusually great.

HABERMAS: Yes, it is.

FLEW: There's a much greater richness of manuscripts for all the major early Christian documents than there is for, say, the plays of Aeschylus or Sophocles or the works of Aristotle. But of course, that's not evidence about Jesus, but very good authority for the accuracy of the text that is printed in translation in the New Testament.

HABERMAS: To answer the first part of your question, though, this is a thing we've disputed for about half an hour now in one form or another. So let me just briefly try to state my position and thereby answer your question. I don't think it's a case of those sources not being written for ten to twenty years after the Crucifixion. Reginald Fuller says that the creed was received by Paul as early as three years after the Crucifixion. A. M. Hunter says six years and Pannenberg says eight years afterward.[1] Now that's when Paul received it. If Peter and James gave it to Paul, which I believe is the thesis of all three of these scholars and a number of others, then the creed itself is earlier still. Then you have to ask how long it was before the actual facts were stylized into a creed. That's my earlier point, which is that we're right back to the time of the Crucifixion itself. I disagree with the thesis that the earliest testimony we have is ten to twenty years later, but even if it were, ten to twenty years later is early testimony. When Dr. Flew was answering questions tonight, he mentioned certain Greek writers. I didn't hear Dr. Flew say that the earliest copies we have of some of Plato's books, for instance, were made one thousand to fifteen hundred years after they were written. We just say, "Plato said." But now he's objecting to ten years. But again, even if ten to twenty years later is the case, I still think that's excellent evidence. But I won't even go along with ten to twenty years. I think the sources date from just after the Crucifixion, and these are from the eyewitnesses themselves.

BECK: Dr. Flew, two questions, please. I believe that you intimated that any evidence that there might have been for the early Resurrection in the Gospel accounts was destroyed in A.D. 70. I was wondering how you knew this. Also, you seem to reject the consensus of scholars on the dating of 1 Corinthians and correspondingly the creeds and other historical data, and yet you accept the dates on the Crucifixion for dating that ten- to twenty-year period. How can you do that?

FLEW: Wait a minute. How am I supposed to have challenged scholars regarding 1 Corinthians? I was simply taking the earliest estimate of the date of 1 Corinthians, which is roughly in the early A.D. 40s, and I was also taking it that the Easter events, whatever they were, were sometime in the early A.D. 30s, and that gives us a ten-year gap, with a possible dispute about what St. Paul got.

BECK: If you accept the dating of the A.D. 30 period, why do you not accept the consensus of critical scholars of the early dating of 1 Corinthians and the creeds?

FLEW: But wait a minute. What is this consensus? I mean, I haven't challenged the dating of 1 Corinthians, I've simply asked the people who have a recognized estimate in the field what is the minimum respectable earliest date that is seriously argued for, and I've taken it as that. There's a great difference between the dating of the text of 1 Corinthians and the dating of some event or some document or some statement mentioned in 1 Corinthians.

MIETHE: Don't you need the date of one to establish the time period of the other?

FLEW: Well, of course, if something is said in 1 Corinthians to have occurred so many years before I wrote 1 Corinthians, then it is desirable if you want to find the date of what was said to have occurred in years before the date of 1 Corinthians to know the date of 1 Corinthians. Clearly, if the author's statement is true, the date is not going to be later than the date of 1 Corinthians, it's going to be many years earlier than that. So of course you need the date of 1 Corinthians if you're trying to determine the disputed date of something earlier than 1 Corinthians.

MIETHE: Okay, and Dr. Habermas, I'd like for you to respond to that, and also to something Dr. Flew brought up earlier, something I thought was curious concerning if there was a supernatural resurrection of someone who was as dead as dead could be. How do you know that Jesus was dead as dead can be? Or was he?

HABERMAS: To respond to the earlier question you asked Dr. Flew, I think he's still not coming to grips with the fact that Paul received the creed in the A.D. 30s. Paul was not reporting secondary sources, because the creed is not even his material; he was probably given this by the eyewitnesses themselves. Also, Dr. Flew had admitted that he doesn't want to propose a naturalistic theory. So if you've got Paul receiving the material from the eyewitnesses, and naturalistic theories don't work, I think that's good evidence for what the eyewitnesses taught. I think he is still not facing the kind of facts that have convinced a large number, maybe a majority, of contemporary theologians. It's a powerful argument, not arrived at by fundamentalists, but by critical scholars. The basic facts concerning this creed are agreed to by virtually everybody. To answer your other question, how do we know that Jesus was dead as dead can be? Very quickly, I'll give you an outlined list of evidences. First, we know from the nature of crucifixion that it is not something from which you can just walk away. Death by crucifixion was essentially death by asphyxiation. This is verified by the skeleton of a crucifixion victim named John found in 1968. John was crucified in the first century. His ankles were broken, which is an indication of the asphyxiation. They didn't just get down off the cross alive, unless that was the specific intention of the executioners. Second, we're told that Jesus was already dead, so the Roman soldiers didn't break his ankles. But he was stabbed in the chest with a spear, anyway, and blood and water came out. There has been much medical interest in this description, and the chief explanation is that the blood came from the right side of the heart and the water came from the pericardium. In other words, if Jesus was still alive, the spear wound would have killed him. We also have an ancient Roman author who says that it was typical crucifixion procedure to pierce the victim with a spear to make sure the person was dead.[2] So the Gospel testimony is corroborated at this point, revealing a high probability that Jesus was dead. Third, I think that if the Shroud of Turin is Jesus' (which hasn't even been mentioned by Dr. Flew, interestingly enough), then it provides more strong evidence for Jesus' death. The man buried in the shroud exhibits postmortem blood flow and he's in a state of rigor mortis. If the man is Jesus, then we have two proofs that he's dead. And last, David Strauss's critique, as I said in my initial paper, killed the swoon theory 150 years ago in 1835. In his major study on nineteenth-century theology, Albert Schweitzer said that David Strauss's critique destroyed such naturalistic theorization, and Schweitzer listed no proponents of the swoon theory after 1840.[3] The first hurdle was for Jesus to have done all the fantastic things that the swoon theorists said he's supposed to have done—he didn't die on the Cross, even though all the medical knowledge is against it; he lay in the tomb without food or water; he rolled the stone away; if there was a guard there, he fought the guard off; he walked blocks to where the disciples were; and so on. But Strauss, the radical New Testament critic, said that even if all of this happened, there's still a major problem with the swoon theory.[4] Here's the main problem with the scenario. Jesus wished to appear to the disciples, so he opened the door and walked inside. Now he had not been raised, so what shape would he be in? He would be bleeding from his wounds, limping, he'd be pale, blood would be dripping behind him —this is only (by our calendar) perhaps two days later, from Friday to Sunday. So he would be in bad shape, and he would walk in the door, and say to his disciples, "Fellows, I'm the crucified and raised Lord of life." And they're going to believe him? As Strauss concluded in 1835, they would get a doctor, not proclaim him risen.[5] And as I've been saying lately in some of my lectures, I can just see the disciples looking at Jesus, bleeding, pale, crippled, and saying, "Oh boy, I can't wait until I get a Resurrection body just like his!" So the chief weakness is that even if Jesus swooned, he couldn't have convinced the disciples that he was risen. I'll say this in defense of Dr. Flew, however, he has not even hinted that he would hold the swoon theory. This theory was discredited 150 years ago. There is good evidence that Jesus was dead, dead, dead.

FLEW: I wasn't intending to suggest by "dead as dead can be" that I was an adherent of this particular theory. Habermas and I are in entire agreement about that being rubbish.

MIETHE: Gentlemen, you each have two minutes for a closing statement. May I suggest that much has been made during this debate of the number of years, say seven years, eight years, or ten years, beyond the events for the records. The claim has been made consistently that that time frame, in the context of modern psychic research, is much too long for the claims to be investigated properly. Yet is it not true that whether it's seven years, eight years, or ten years, the claim was that the body was no longer there, that all the eyewitnesses were still alive, and that the church was causing so much trouble with its claim that the Roman government certainly could have put this to a rest by producing contrary evidence? Would you address that, Dr. Flew and Dr. Habermas, for two minutes each, please. Dr. Flew.

FLEW: Yes, well. The 1 Corinthians statement has nothing about empty tombs and such. And there's a difference between offering a theory that fails to fit the facts and saying that we don't know enough facts to offer a theory. I think it is fundamentally wrong to take it that we know enough about what was going on at Easter in Jerusalem to offer a plausible rival account of it. We're just not in a position to reconstruct from the evidence we've got a tolerable account of what was going on there.

HABERMAS: Dr. Flew has said, I think for the first time tonight, that Paul does not report the empty tomb in the creed in 1 Corinthians 15. But in verses 3 and 4, Paul says that Christ was dead, in the grave, and then raised. This strongly implies an empty tomb, especially for a Jewish audience, because the Resurrection of the body was the common view. Additionally, how could Jesus' Resurrection have been successfully proclaimed in Jerusalem if his body could have been produced? This type of argumentation has been recognized frequently in contemporary theology. Craig lists forty-four critical scholars who argue for the empty tomb.[6]

Second, Dr. Flew said that he didn't offer a naturalistic theory of the Resurrection. Well, he mentioned the hallucination theory twice, and the hallucination theory has been thoroughly refuted by scholars. He admits that the apostles did not see hallucinations, and I argued earlier that I think it's also wrong to apply this hypothesis to Paul. He's got to use Acts 9, 22, and 26 to argue about any details of the appearance to Paul. But to argue from these chapters, I think, will show that hallucination doesn't work for Paul either.

But third, Dr. Flew said that we do not have enough facts to know what happened. Again, I think Dr. Flew's problem is that we do have enough facts to know, but because he doesn't have a viable naturalistic theory he has to say something like he did. I don't think we can say, "The facts are too cloudy." In my initial paper, the very intent of the core facts argument was to point out that even if you utilize only the facts that the critics admit, you have enough of a basis to say that the eyewitnesses saw Jesus. Dr. Flew has even granted that the earliest disciples believed they saw the risen Jesus. But naturalistic theories don't work, as he also admitted. So aren't we getting very close to a Resurrection now? The eyewitnesses believed they saw the risen Jesus and said so early on, but naturalistic theories don't work. Additionally, all the evidence we do have is in favor of them actually seeing Jesus. Let me conclude by saying this. Recently in Dallas, Dr. Flew turned to the theists that he was debating and said, "Gentlemen, I want some evidence for the existence of God." He went on to say, "I don't need conclusive evidence, but please give me some sort of evidence." Then, in an especially impassioned speech, he turned to us in the crowd and said,

"I'll take *any* evidence for God's existence." Tonight I think I provided some strong evidences for the historicity of the Resurrection, but Dr. Flew has not responded to any of the four sets of evidences for this event. He has not come up with a naturalistic theory, he has not disproven the positive evidences, he has not answered the core facts (and has even admitted these crucial points), and he has said nothing about the Shroud of Turin. So although I realize that he has said a lot of things, what he hasn't given me is evidence. So, Dr. Flew, I paraphrase to you what you said to the theists in Dallas. Give me some evidence, *any* evidence against the Resurrection. I've not heard any tonight!

NOTES

1. See the sources by Fuller, Hunter, and Pannenberg listed in endnotes 40–42 that follow my debate presentation. Cf. also Fuller, *The Foundations of New Testament Christology*, (New York: Scribner, 1955), 142.
2. Quintillian *Declamationes maiores* 6, 9.
3. See Albert Schweitzer, *The Quest of the Historical Jesus*, trans. W. Montgomery (New York: Macmillan, 1968), 56.
4. For a more complete treatment of the swoon theory and such refutations, see Gary R. Habermas, *Ancient Evidence for the Life of Jesus: Historical Records of His Death and Resurrection* (Nashville: Nelson, 1984), 54–58.
5. David Strauss, *A New Life of Jesus*, vol. 1 (London: Williams and Norgate, 1879), 412.
6. William Lane Craig, *The Son Rises: Historical Evidence for the Resurrection of Jesus* (Chicago: Moody, 1981), 85.

II. THE CONTINUING DEBATE

Discussion: Antony G. N. Flew, Gary R. Habermas, Terry L. Miethe, and W. David Beck

MIETHE: Tony, having had time to reflect on the subject of the Resurrection and our debate of last evening, would you like to make a statement to start our conversation in regard to the conclusions you believe can be drawn from what we have said thus far. In other words, what did you think came out of the debate that was valuable? Have you had any reflections on the debate?

FLEW: Well, I think the main thing that comes out of the debate that is valuable is to have started this thing at all. As I understand it, there has not been any similar published debate about this issue, which we all agree to be of enormous importance, in this country for twenty or so years. It seems to me that the great point of this exercise is that we have had a sort of confrontation from which one hopes that discussion will continue. This is not really a contribution to our discussion. It is really a reviewer's comment on it. But looking at the debate the day after, this is my first thought.

MIETHE: That is precisely why we are here this evening, Tony, to continue the debate. Were there any crucial weaknesses that you perceived were more important than others in the positive argument for the Resurrection?

FLEW: There were several things that I think were not being appreciated as clearly as they should be and that one will want to get straight somewhere along the line. One thing that I am sure would not be a subject of disagreement, but does need to be brought out sharply for a reader, is the difference between evidence about the life of Jesus and evidence about what people believed about Jesus in the church in the A.D. second century. The fact that there is a remarkable amount of non-Christian evidence about what Christians believed and did starting at the beginning roughly of the second century, is no great help for the issue that was concerning us last night. The issue I was raising last evening during the debate was the deplorable lack of non-Christian evidence about the ministry of Jesus, about the Easter events, and indeed about what went on in the first crucial years of the Christian church. There is a significant lack of available evidence on the first crucial years. Yet from the A.D. second century we have a remarkable richness of evidence. But I think one needs to appreciate that this abundance of evidence about what Christians believed is not any great help if what we are considering is what Jesus did.

MIETHE: Gary, what conclusions do you believe were drawn in the debate last evening?

HABERMAS: Let me start by making a brief comment about what Tony has just said. I agree with him to a certain extent about his last statement. The eighteen sources that I mentioned last night as extrabiblical sources for the life of Jesus, as I said at the time, are late when compared, for instance, with the earliest creedal statements. They have that weakness; as a matter of fact, the book I just wrote on that subject draws this same conclusion in the appropriate chapter. [Gary R. Habermas, *Ancient Evidence for the Life of Jesus: Historical Records of His Death and Resurrection* (Nashville: Thomas Nelson, 1984)] They are a bit later.

Just to reiterate an earlier point, however, eighteen sources for one ancient subject is an incredible amount. Additionally, even though these eighteen are later than our other sources for the Resurrection, they are still much closer to the events that they report than are the sources for many highly respected portions of ancient history. Sherwin-White and Grant attest to these large time differences between ancient historical writings and many well-accepted events that they record.[1]

Let me focus on a different issue now. I would answer your question by saying that I think some things came out in our head-to-head discussion that interested me very much. I was surprised that Tony admitted (or at least he appeared to me to admit) several things that were of great interest to me. If I am not mistaken, he said at least twice that the disciples saw visions of Jesus. And when I asked about hallucinations, he said that he did not hold that the disciples saw hallucinations. So those are two examples of some things that I thought were good points: the disciples saw visions, but the visions were not hallucinations. I think we agreed that the creed is a much earlier source than those extrabiblical sources that we were talking about just a moment ago. So the report was early. And then Tony mentioned that there were no valid naturalistic hypotheses, and that he was not going to present any alternative theories himself. I think that was a very important point. And last, Tony admitted that it was at least possible that the Resurrection was a supernatural event. I think he responded to a question by saying that it was not his purpose to rule out the possibility of a supernatural Resurrection in an a priori manner, and I appreciated that. So those are some of the crucially important points that Tony admitted: the disciples saw visions, these were not hallucinations, he would not espouse a naturalistic hypothesis, the Resurrection was proclaimed early, and a supernatural act was at least possible.

Let me draw the conclusion that although Tony probably did not mean to do so, I think that he came as close as possible, for a naturalist, to admitting a literal Resurrection, although he was not trying to do so. I am not saying that Tony believes in the Resurrection of Jesus. But what he admitted to surrounding this event was, to me, surprising. It is a type of core facts argument that we see at work here. If the disciples saw visions that were not hallucinations, if other naturalistic theories do not hold, and the reports are early, I think that very strong evidence is being stated here. I think this is very close to a literal Resurrection, even though I am not saying that Tony believes in the Resurrection.

MIETHE: Let us reverse roles for a second. Often Christians are put in the position of seeming to say that everything David Hume said was wrong, and that we do not agree with Hume on anything he said in regard to miracles. Gary, address what you think was right in Hume, what you support in Hume. Then, Tony, because you mentioned last night in the debate that you did not always agree with Hume, tell us where you disagree with him.

HABERMAS: I generally think that David Hume's essay "On Miracles" makes some fine points on an investigation of claimed supernatural events. Let us just start at the end of Section One. Two paragraphs before the end, Hume gives a definition of miracles. I generally agree with his definition, but I would drop the word *violation* and add a word such as *supersede*. And I would add a statement at the end saying that the purpose of a miracle is to verify a message. Outside of that, I do not strongly disagree with Hume's definition of miracles. In fact, I usually work in the context of his definition.

I also believe, with Hume, that a wise person chooses probabilities. If we are going to believe something, we ought to have good reasons for believing it and not just believe something because it feels good or because we prefer it to be a certain way. I agree with Hume that in most cases when miracle-claims are investigated, they are not justifiable claims to knowledge. I also think Hume is generally right in several of his four subpoints in Section Two of the essay, where he says, for instance, that extraordinary events are gossiped about; they often tend to get bigger and bigger as time goes on, and people sometimes repeat them in a noncritical manner. I guess there is a list of about a half-dozen things in Hume's essay that I think are positive and I think I could probably find the same things in Tony's writings, the same kind of cautions before you accept some events as historical. We obviously disagree on the Resurrection, but I would agree with those kind of cautions.

MIETHE: Now, Tony, did you not say last evening that there were some problems with Hume's approach?

FLEW: Oh gosh, yes! I think there are a lot of faults in that section of *An Enquiry Concerning the Human Understanding.* I mentioned two of the major ones. One is that Hume has disqualified himself from giving any account of natural possibility or natural impossibility, and there-fore disqualified himself from employing the notion of a miracle in a strong interpretation. I am happy to change the word, and I use the word *overriding,* an overriding of the law of nature. The other thing is that Hume was, of course, going to become one of the leading historians, but it was in the early eighteenth century that he started writing history, and he was unsophisticated about these matters, as were his contemporaries. He was inclined to assume that there was virtually no space between accepting that some witness was giving an accurate account of what actually happened and saying that the witness was deliberately lying. I think for considering the evidence in a complex case such as this, where virtually all the major people are people who are above suspicion of deliberate distortion, it is important to emphasize that there is a lot of room between these two extremes.

You say that you can accept Hume's definition. I am not surprised, because Hume's definition was the one that was being used by his opponents in the controversies, almost word for word. Samuel Clark, for example, was a leading Christian apologist and wrote a famous set of lectures for the rational defense of the Christian faith. He was also the man who acted as Newton's intermediary in the Leibniz-Clark correspondence. So Hume was, in fact, taking a definition. The word *violation* may have been something that Hume contributed, but the essence of the matter, as opposed to the emotional overtones, was in Samuel Clark.

Regarding the other things you were saying earlier, I am afraid you exaggerate our agreement. I do not see a clear distinction between visions and hallucinations. I take it that someone who is having a vision is having an experience that is like that of seeing something in front of them when there is not actually something in front of them. Of course there may be different degrees of vividness and thus different degrees of conviction in the person as to whether they are seeing something. I suppose we would call it a hallucination when they believe that the thing was actually there. Maybe the distinction is that they call it a vision when they do not believe that this is a case of normal seeing. Is that the sort of thing you have in mind?

HABERMAS: Do you or do you not believe that the disciples saw hallucinations?

FLEW: I believe that they had some sort of experience. I think the most likely thing is that they had some sort of vision experience similar to St. Paul's experience. But they did not see something that was actually out there in front of them.

HABERMAS: So it was not an objective vision? It was not an actual vision of the risen Jesus?

FLEW: No, not of any mind-independent reality. But I take it that they believed they actually saw a spiritual being.

HABERMAS: Is there a marked difference between that and a hallucination? I think not.

BECK: One of the areas left dangling after the debate is that Gary accused you several times, Tony, of in fact holding some version of the hallucination theory. You seemed at several points to object to that and yet you did seem to offer some account of how the stories got started and an account in terms of something like the disciples, in fact, having some sort of experience. You called it a vision or something. I think we have to focus in on that and see just where the difference is, and in particular just how you, Tony, account for what the disciples believed.

FLEW: Well, I go through two stages about this. There is a question of accounting for how the people from whom we do have direct statements came to believe that a Resurrection had occurred.

BECK: You have already answered that.

FLEW: There are different answers with different people. I am not taking for granted that all the Resurrection appearances described in the Gospels actually occurred. The way I take it, the problem is to explain how Christians, or how the first people to believe that a Resurrection had occurred, came to believe that. The first person whose testimony we actually have directly is St. Paul. He did not claim to have seen something that was measurable by instruments or visible to other people who happened to be around. There is no reason to doubt that he had some sort of visual experience, and the analogy I kept using was the vision that Bernadette had. Of course I do not think anyone was claiming that had the movie cameras been there they would have been able to record Bernadette's vision. Does that give the answer?

MIETHE: No, part of the question was, "How do you account for that?"

FLEW: I do not imagine that there was any external cause. But I think that those people who took it that they had had visions of the risen Jesus believed, as it seems to me St. Paul believed, that they were actually seeing a peculiar sort of object. I imagine that his notion of a spiritual body was probably something like the notion of an astral body used by spiritualists. They take it that an astral body will not be visible to normal people who do not have psychic powers, but may become visible if you are in a specially privileged situation. They do believe that there is something objectively there. So that would be my interpretation of St. Paul's evidence, which I regard as the absolutely crucial thing, because his is the first eyewitness statement by someone who claims to have had contact with the risen Jesus, and who also claims (and there is no reason to deny this) that this is what made him a Christian. This is what St. Paul is saying, it was this Resurrection experience that made him a Christian.

BECK: All right, you also said that you did not think that the disciples, and I assume you are including Paul, lied in any sense.

FLEW: Oh gosh, no.

BECK: Part of my question was, How do we explain the fact that they came to describe these experiences in normal observational kind of language? I think especially of the first verses in the first epistle of John, where John uses some strongly objective observational terms. Also, why would they come to the point of having to infiltrate their accounts with predictions of this bodily Resurrection made by Jesus himself, because one would have had to put that in afterward. I am trying to account now for the total picture of your scheme of things. Then I need Gary to also respond.

FLEW: I do not think a total picture can be produced, because you are taking it that we have the evidence of the people whose experiences are recorded in the Gospels, but we merely have the stories that these things happened to other people, not their eyewitness stories.

BECK: Let us assume we do not, in fact, know what they saw, but we do at least have their account. That is all I am asking you to explain.

FLEW: But that is what I do not think we have. We do not have accounts. Here we have a story that the twelve saw Jesus. We do not have stories from the members of that body. Surely we do not, do we? Does anyone believe that any of the Gospels were written by people who were original disciples?

BECK: I think many would certainly argue that all of the four accounts are eyewitness accounts or at least traceable and authorized by eyewitnesses.

HABERMAS: Many would argue that if they were not written by eyewitnesses, eyewitness sources are behind them.

FLEW: Oh yes, but once you have got two stages of the game, there is much more room for distortions and theorization. A distortion does not necessarily mean dishonest distortion. One of the things I was making quite a big thing of during the debate was how easy it is for people who have been involved in a theory, and are puzzling about the significance of an experience, to interpret the experience in light of their various general beliefs about the world. We know that all the people urgently concerned were Jews. They were people who were inclined to see prophecies of contemporary events in the Jewish Bible. This means, musing about this over a long time, you begin to say, "Well now, this was surely a fulfillment of that prophecy. It must have been like this, wasn't it. I must have been mistaken in thinking it was like that."

When you have two layers of these people, then you have to say the author, who is writing on the basis of accounts and all concerned have been thinking like that, can get a very different story at the end without anyone doing anything other than inquiring about a thing with a serious concern for the truth. After all, they all believed that these were prophetic writings and the prophecies would be fulfilled in their era if they got it right.

HABERMAS: I have two fundamental disagreements with some things that Tony just said, and the first goes back to our head-to-head discussion. The first thing is that you keep saying we do not have any reports from the twelve that they saw the resurrected Jesus. But we went over this many times last night. Paul received the report, between A.D. 33 and A.D. 38 from the eyewitnesses. Most critical theologians who address the issue hold that Paul was given this material by Peter and James in Jerusalem. They were eyewitnesses and both are listed in the creed in 1 Corinthians 15. Now if they gave the creed to Paul, then that is a step earlier than the date of A.D. 33 to A.D. 38, which is when Paul received it. If they gave it to him, they knew it even earlier. And then the facts that make up the creed before it is stylized have to be even earlier. So we have three stages, the facts themselves, the disciples' formulation of it, and Paul's receiving of it. We do have the eyewitness material here because it was the eyewitnesses, in all likelihood, who gave it to Paul, number one. Second, in 1 Corinthians 15:11, 14, and 15, right after the creed, Paul states that these same eyewitnesses were also proclaiming this message that Jesus was raised. So we do have the eyewitness reports.

MIETHE: Proclaiming it at the same time Paul did.

HABERMAS: Yes, other disciples were teaching it at the same time that Paul was proclaiming it. So without even using the Gospel argument that was referred to earlier, we have two arguments that say the eyewitnesses did give the reports. Number one, the creed that they gave Paul, and number two, Paul says that they were concurrently reporting the same thing. So we have got them giving him the creed and we have got them preaching the same message.

My second disagreement is that I have not noticed any difference between your vision theory, Tony, and a hallucination theory. If something impinges on your senses and it is objectively there, then that is not a hallucination. Or if I see this chair but I think it is a dog, that is also not a hallucination, because I am really seeing the chair. If I wake up in the middle of the night and I think someone is standing in my room, but it is my hat placed on top of the television, that is an illusion. But if I see something for which there is no objective or external stimuli, as you stated, Tony, then it seems to me that is the same thing as a hallucination.

FLEW: Yes, all right. I do not make a sharp distinction between visions and hallucinations. I am prepared to make a distinction in terms of the beliefs of the experiencer. I think that there probably is a nuance here that psychologists would employ; for it to be a hallucination, the person must believe that they are seeing something and not just have the experience as if they are seeing. So you could make a distinction here.

HABERMAS: So did the disciples see hallucinations or not?

FLEW: I suppose it would be right to say hallucination insofar as they believed they were seeing something. But, of course, it is going to be tricky, because it is a marginal case. If they believed what Paul, after the event, seems to have believed about it (and there is no particular reason to think that they did believe this), namely, that what he was seeing was not an ordinary physical body but a spiritual body, then it would seem to me that the difference you are wanting to make between a hallucination and a vision is beginning to collapse here in this special case of visions that are construed as visions of spiritual bodies. It seems to be terribly like hallucinations, because the spiritual body is thought to be a really existing spiritual body. Whereas in a hallucination you think you are seeing a really existing physical body.

HABERMAS: To me it does not make any difference whether it is a physical or a spiritual vision; if it is a hallucination, it is a hallucination. We both agree that hallucinations have no objective reference. So I think you just said a minute ago that you would put the disciples' experience, roughly, in the category of hallucinations. Now you have got to answer the same questions that caused the hallucination theory to become unpopular with the advent of modern psychology and psychiatry. I read you a scholarly quotation last night that said that for anyone to prove that more than one person saw a hallucination, they would have to go against much of the current psychiatric and psychological data about the nature of hallucinations. So we have a refutation such as the creed, which states that the twelve saw Jesus, and a little later we are told that the apostles also saw Jesus. Two people cannot see a hallucination, let alone twelve or more people. That is a major problem, beside the many others.

FLEW: Oh no, I entirely agree. But I was not saying this as my account of alleged collective experience here. I was talking about the Pauline experience, which is the experience for which I think that there is the most solid evidence. But about the creed, I was wondering whether to reach for my Gideon Bible last night at the debate but in the end did not. I think we haven't got one around. I cannot give you the creed from memory. I imagine Terry's got a Bible stashed away somewhere.

The thing here is, I think you all along were taking it that the first creed contained the verses giving St. Paul's list of the appearances known to him. I took it that the creed did not contain that material at all. Unless you have got some independent evidence, you do not have to read this as being just a reiteration of an accepted creed, but it is his evidence for believing a crucial element in the creed.

HABERMAS: According to the New Testament scholars who work on this subject, everyone begins the creed with verse 3, because Paul says, "For I delivered to you as of first importance what I also received, that Christ died for our sins in accordance with the scriptures, that he was buried, that he was raised on the third day in accordance with the scriptures, and that he appeared to Cephas, then to the twelve." Now that, minimum, is the creed. Then many scholars believe that one or more of the following verses are also the creed: "After that, he was seen of about five hundred brethren at once; of whom the greater part remain to the present, but some are fallen asleep. After that he was seen by James; then by all the Apostles." So some scholars take the creed as being chapter 15, verses 3 to 7, but some take the creed as being only verses 3 to 5. But even if you go only as far as verse 5, you still have two appearances reported by the eyewitness creed, first to Peter and then to the twelve disciples. It seems to me that is a crucial problem for the hallucination theory, because an appearance to the twelve is in that list. That was what I kept hitting last night. And because this group appearance is in the creed, even if we take the shorter creed and quit at verse 5, we still have an eyewitness report of a collective experience —an appearance to the twelve.

Here is an example of some problems for hallucination theorists: (1) two people cannot see a hallucination, let alone twelve; (2) there were many different time and place factors involved in the appearances; (3)

in order to have a hallucination, one believes something so strongly that one's mind produces the picture. But one of the facts I mentioned last night, accepted by virtually everybody, is that the disciples were in a state of despair after the death of Jesus, and thus did not believe that Jesus was going to rise from the dead. So the psychological preconditions for a hallucination were also lacking. Here are three problems, and there are many others. So, as I said, even if you argue only through the fifth verse, you are going to have a major problem.

I read a quote last night, so I will not read the whole thing again, but this is a quote from a well-published clinical psychologist, who states that, "Hallucinations are individual occurrences. By their very nature, only one person can see a given hallucination at a time. They certainly are not something which can be seen by a group of people. Neither is it possible that one person could somehow induce an hallucination in somebody else." Then this last sentence: "Since an hallucination exists only in this subjective, personal sense, it is obvious that others cannot witness it."[2] So now I go back to my point that if there are twelve people in the creed who see the risen Jesus, it cannot be a hallucination. But again, you are fluctuating between whether it is Paul who saw a hallucination or the disciples who saw a hallucination. I think there are some good reasons why Paul did not see a hallucination, but I am saying it absolutely does not work with the disciples.

MIETHE: Tony, most New Testament scholars point out that one of the ways we know it is a creedal statement is that it appears to have been in a more primitive Aramaic, and it's also in hymnic form. This means it was stylized Greek, non-Pauline words, and so on, which indicates that it predated Paul and was widely used, probably even used and recited in worship experiences as a form of worship or a song or a hymn or a creedal statement, and was therefore universally acknowledged. Now, what do you say to these three problems that Gary has raised for hallucinations?

FLEW: Well, I have neither denied nor suggested that collective hallucinations are impossible, but I'm going one step at a time, always working with the thing for which there is the really strong evidence, which is the vision of St. Paul. I suppose an indirect way of coming at this is that the disciples were supposed to be in despair. I do not see on what basis all these scholars think they know the disciples were in despair. I point out that most of these scholars believe that the disciples had what they interpreted as clear statements that their master was in fact the God of Abraham, Isaac, and Israel.

You might well say that the disciples were half-witted if they believed that the Crucifixion was final. They ought not to have been in despair if events actually occurred as reported. They ought to have been sitting around waiting for something to happen. If, say, the things that Matthew reports about the tearing of the veil of the temple and the earthquake actually happened, the disciples would not have been in despair. Even at the minimum, if the Resurrection predictions had been given by their teacher, if he'd said he was going to be put to death and was going to rise, why should the believers despair, when so far the prophecies have come true? He has been executed, he said he was going to rise after he had been executed. How are we supposed to know that they were in despair?

MIETHE: You are admitting, then, that a dozen people can hallucinate at the same time?

FLEW: You talk as if you were getting a confession out of me.

MIETHE: No, do you think it is possible? I am not asking for a confession.

FLEW: No, I have always understood that mass or collective hallucinations really cannot happen. This has sometimes been suggested as an explanation of the so-called miracle of Fatima, and I have always understood that this was not a mass hallucination. But you are always doing the thing that I think is fundamentally unsound and impossible. You're taking the Gospel documents as if these were things that had been written down in Jerusalem at the time, then saying, Now how on earth do you fit these pieces together to give a consistent naturalistic account? I do not try to fit these pieces together, because I think most of these pieces are pieces we have not got a good reason for believing in anyway.

HABERMAS: I am going to note several problems that I have with what you have just said. It appears that one of the main responses you keep making is that the Gospels are not eyewitness sources, therefore we cannot really trust what they say, and that Paul is the only eyewitness account we have, so we have to go to Paul. I must repeat that it does make a difference that there is eyewitness testimony behind the Gospels. This is argued by Raymond Brown, A. M. Hunter, John A. T. Robinson, F. F. Bruce, and a number of reputable scholars[3] who have occupied chairs of critical exegesis in New Testament at well-known universities. And if there is eyewitness testimony behind the Gospels, that makes an enormous difference.

But this is not the argument I have stressed either last night or tonight. I have stressed an entirely different line that bypasses this point. My argument says that the facts that even the critics admit, the facts that believers and skeptics can agree on, are enough to show that the disciples were correct in their claim that Jesus was literally raised from the dead. And you, Tony, keep going back to the Gospels as if just to cite them is the issue. But my argument is chiefly concerned with the creedal evidence, and especially 1 Corinthians 15:3ff. I repeat my claim that the eyewitnesses do report the creed; it is not Paul's material. We have to remember something: Paul would not have had the creed had he not been told by somebody. Who gave Paul the creed? Again, the leading conclusion is that he received it from Peter and James in Jerusalem. So (1) we have eyewitness testimony actually reported in the creed because the eyewitnesses gave it to Paul; and (2) unless we want to say that Paul was totally mistaken—and you, Tony, said you did not want to do that, and I do not know anybody else who does—Paul says that the actual eyewitnesses were reporting the same message, that is, that Jesus was literally raised from the dead. Paul states this right after the creed, in verses 11, 14, and 15.

To answer your other question, How do we know the disciples were in despair? You said that because they really believed Jesus was God, they would be nuts to believe that the Cross was the end. I think you are making a fundamental error here in New Testament thought, because the disciples did not believe this about Jesus before the Cross, at least not clearly. As I said last night, the disciples, as did a great many early first-century Christians, looked back at the claims of Jesus through the Cross and the Resurrection. I would not want to give statistics, but I would think that most New Testament scholars today realize that most of the early first-century Christians became Christians after the Resurrection. The Resurrection had a major effect on first-century belief. So in between the Cross and the Resurrection they did not conclude, "This man is God and therefore cannot be dead." It was not the post-*Cross* experience that gave rise to faith, it was the *Resurrection* appearances that gave rise to faith. You can say that the disciples did not despair only by proving a significant amount of pre-Resurrection faith, and I do not know anybody who is willing to do that.

MIETHE: It is clear in the New Testament that the apostles did not understand Jesus to be making the claim to his own Resurrection, but to the rebuilding of the temple, should it be destroyed. They thought that the temple was what he said would be torn down and then raised; they were not looking for a bodily Resurrection of Jesus.

FLEW: Well, if that is the case, presumably there was no prophecy of the Resurrection, if what he was saying was the temple would be torn down.

MIETHE: No, that does not logically follow. They simply misunderstood what Jesus was saying. It is quite possible (obvious, in fact) that Jesus was making two illustrations and in fact giving a prophecy, but they misunderstood the prophecy.

FLEW: Yes, it is possible. Are you saying that it is wrong to interpret what is so often said to be the claims to be God, in particular, say, in St. John, as somehow having been read into the story after the event? Because I would think that this was the most probable thing, but I am not sure it is what you were saying.

What are you going to say about Jesus if he claimed to be God? Are you going to say that he was God or he was a madman? This was a classic challenge with which to confront the unbeliever—assuming that certain passages, particularly in John, were the claims uttered by Jesus to his disciples to be, in fact, Jehovah.

BECK: But there does seem to be a point to that. I find your account of how these stories got started and why early Christians believed them to be implausible. I guess that would make sense if what we were talking about was some trivial claim that made no difference to anyone. Suppose this guy comes along and claims to have had a vision of a purple elephant. I suppose one could convince some people that he had in fact done that, and perhaps one could, because it does not really matter to anyone. But we are talking here about something that utterly changed a great many lives and for which eventually a number of people died. So it seems implausible to me that they would have taken this original vision that Paul had, that the disciples and Paul himself would come to describe in completely objective language, not in vision language, and that it would have been accepted by so many as being a truth upon which they came to stake their lives. That does not seem to be a coherent account.

FLEW: Paul does precisely this. It is on the basis of him taking the claim about a vision rather than seeing a physical, detectable person.

BECK: Well, we must get clear as to why you think Paul ever talks about a vision (apart from the King James translation).

FLEW: For a start, he is not claiming to have used his hands to feel the vision. He is not making the crucial test of mind-independent reality. He is also going on in 1 Corinthians 15, on and on about corruption and incorruption and spiritual bodies and how wrong it is to believe that the Resurrection would involve an ordinary, run-of-the-mill, corruptible, physical body.

BECK: Well, he may not use tactile observation terms, but he certainly uses other kinds of observation terms, such as the word for "seeing."

FLEW: Yes, but this is what those who believe in astral bodies are going to say, because they think that there is something there that they think of as a spiritual body.

HABERMAS: Rather than argue my own view, let me pursue your point about astral bodies. If twelve people cannot see a hallucination at one time, how do we know that the disciples or Paul did not see a literal but glorified, astral body of Jesus? It is almost as if you, Tony, reject any type of literal body in an a priori manner. Now I know you do not want to argue a priori, so how do we know that this body they saw could not have been a literal body, of whatever composition?

FLEW: Well, I do not claim the notion of an astral body is a viable notion that I am trying to make intelligible. This talk about spiritual bodies comes from St. Paul, not from me; I would never propose that someone had seen a spiritual body. But I was asked the question, How do you interpret this particular evidence? You keep bringing in the thing about the twelve as if I had said that I wanted to account for both St. Paul's experience and an experience had by all twelve collectively in the same way. On the contrary, I do not think that we have got adequate evidence that all the twelve did see anything collectively. This is a stunning claim.

HABERMAS: The creed is an early report by eyewitnesses that the twelve saw the risen Jesus. You have got to get around that somehow.

FLEW: That is a very different thing from having a report that comes from them.

HABERMAS: It did come from them.

FLEW: I just do not see the evidence as being good enough. It is not printed in the text in Aramaic. A Greek testament does not include this in Aramaic. It does not make any distinction.

You have got a problem on your hands. Why is it that the first Christian creed contains what is thought to be evidential backing? None of the classic creeds in the books of devotion contain this sort of thing. It is very odd to think that the first creed was different from all later creeds.

HABERMAS: Let me try to explain both questions. You said the creed is obviously not written in Aramaic, because the New Testament is in Greek and Paul wrote 1 Corinthians in Greek. Okay, nobody is claiming that that passage is in Aramaic. Joachim Jeremias, Reginald Fuller and others have presented some evidence that has been accepted by a number of scholars that Paul recorded the creed in Greek, but that it may have been originally transmitted in Aramaic.⁴ Nobody says that the creed in the text is actually in Aramaic. Let me just give you a couple examples of where this conclusion comes from. For instance, Paul says, "I delivered unto you that which I also received." These are obviously Greek words, but the words *delivered* and *received* are the equivalent of technical rabbinic words for receiving and passing on tradition. Second, notice that Paul uses the Aramaic name for Peter; he calls him Cephas. Now Paul does this on other occasions, but it is still a consideration. So, again, to qualify that, the creed is not in Aramaic, but the claim by Jeremias and Cullmann is that the creed was originally in Aramaic and in our form it is in the Greek translation. Just like this is an English translation of the Greek New Testament. What was your second question?

FLEW: That is not nearly good enough to hinge something important on, that all these were parts of the creed. Of course the prefatory stuff about having received this that I am passing on, and of course the actual things about Christ's Resurrection, this I think is clearly part of some sort of creed. After all, these phrases are found in the Nicene Creed and the Athanasian Creed. It is the inclusion of the evidence from Cephas onward that I question. One of the things I made a lot about last night in the debate was that if this was part of the first actual creed that all the first converts recited, saying, "the first appearance was to Peter," it is very odd that not merely is this creed lost without recovery and replaced later on by quite different creeds that do not contain the evidence, but none of the Gospels make the appearance to Peter the first appearance. The only reference to the appearance to Peter, as opposed to the other disciples, is in, is it in Luke?

HABERMAS: Luke 24:34.

FLEW: Now, these are very odd things.

HABERMAS: Okay, now we have got two more questions, one regarding Peter and one regarding the apologetics in this creed. Luke does report that there was an appearance to Peter. But, I will just add parenthetically, the creed does not say that the first appearance was necessarily to Peter. All it says is "he appeared to Peter," and he is placed first on the list. But second, you asked why there are apologetic evidences here but not in other creeds. There are dozens of creedal statements in the New Testament; sometimes they are just a few words long, sometimes they are one verse long, but this one is somewhat longer. Some of them do present evidences along with the teaching.

I will give you an example of another creed with evidence. In Romans 1:3–4, Paul presents a creed, which presents lofty Christological titles. It calls Jesus the Son of God, Christ (Messiah) and Lord. And this creed states that Jesus was declared to be these things—Son of God, Messiah, and Lord—by his Resurrection from the dead. So Paul recites another creed in Romans 1:3–4. By the way, even Bultmann says that Romans 1:3–4 is a creedal statement.[5] So here is an example of another creed where apologetics is used. Jesus was shown to be the Son of God, Messiah, and Lord by the Resurrection. I really do not care whether the Disciple's Creed, the Nicene Creed, or the Chalcedonian Creed give evidences. First of all, they are centuries later, so there is no real comparison. And even in the New Testament, some of the creeds have evidences and some do not. These two I have mentioned do.

FLEW: Yes, but you keep saying these things are creeds, but surely to say that something is a creed, you want to say more than these are expressions of shared beliefs. You want to say that this was some regularly used formula of belief. These scholars are agreeing that these were creeds without having some independent evidence of it. It seems to me that this is a game with no rules, played in a swamp, if you just find a passage expressing fundamental Christian belief in the New Testament and say that this is a creed because it is a creedal statement.

HABERMAS: If all we had was a statement in the New Testament and we did not know where it came from, it would be a game played in a swamp. But this is something I do not think you are answering. I have listed numerous critical scholars, none of whom agree with me theologically, who have said that this is a creedal statement but that it is not a nameless, or placeless, or personless creed. It was reported by Paul after it was received by him in the A.D. 30s, most likely given to him by two eyewitnesses, and they themselves based it on events that they had experienced personally. Now that is the first problem you will have to overcome. It is not just a nameless creed that some Christian church somewhere repeated at a church service.

Now if that is all it was, then I would agree with you that it is hearsay and circumstantial. But that is not what this creed is; this creed is the claim of eyewitnesses to have seen the risen Jesus. Now just because the eyewitnesses claimed to have seen the risen Jesus, it is true that that does not mean they did. But if this creed dates early, and it does, as everybody admits, and if it comes from the eyewitnesses, which is pretty well accepted, then you have got to explain on what grounds we can reject the eyewitness testimony.

You yourself said last night that there are no naturalistic theories that you are going to apply to this event. So, again, we have eyewitnesses. I will repeat this point one more time: if it was only something they recited in a church in some unknown vicinity, this creed would mean comparatively less. But the value of the creed is twofold: it is *early* and it is *eyewitness*. When you have an early, eyewitness creed, you have got to deal with some difficult testimony, because then the naturalistic theories do not apply to it. What are you left with? You said the naturalistic theories do not apply, Tony, so what are you left with?

You are left with eyewitnesses who said they saw the risen Jesus and gave other evidence that this was indeed what actually happened. That testimony has not been explained away. This has been the major argument for convincing a large percentage of present critical New Testament scholarship. I think there is a larger percent of critical New Testament and systematic theologians today believing the literal Resurrection than there has been for probably two centuries. And this is one of the main reasons. I think we have to come to grips with the fact that it is an eyewitness creed, not a nameless creed recited in a nameless church.

FLEW: I think it is perfectly extraordinary that people should hinge a matter of such enormous importance on such a weak piece of evidence. Really, here we have someone who's had an experience of a particular sort. Paul is reporting that these things occurred. We assumed that he talked—he does claim, doesn't he, elsewhere—to have talked with two of the apostles. And you are calling this eyewitness testimony to various things, including a collective vision by all twelve of them. Well, if you were not the deity, but you yourself, wanting to make a revelation about Liberty University, wouldn't you provide better evidence than this? Especially if there was a miracle to be believed in on the basis of this revelation. A couple of chaps whom we cannot cross-examine are reported to have said it.

HABERMAS: You could cross-examine the evidence. And it is falsifiable if there is a naturalistic theory that can be proven. Let us use this example: you come to Dave and I and we tell you that we have had an eyewitness experience of something. Now later Terry wants to disprove this, because you are proclaiming it now. We told you we saw it . . .

FLEW: No, wait a minute, it is not the eyewitness experience I am disputing. It is the claim that is essentially involved in this, that they actually saw something there. Now we are going to say, "I have got to believe in the pink elephants because someone tells me that he met someone who swore that he became blinded seeing pink elephants."

BECK: I think there is one more issue that has got to be solved in relation to Paul, and then it is obvious that we must go on to the other disciples. The issue is the statement in Paul about a spiritual body, because it seems to me that is at the heart of what is still hindering the evidence from Paul. My question is this: I am not clear why we are so obsessed with the term *spiritual body*. The only place it has any importance is here in 1 Corinthians 15.

Paul is using the term *spiritual body* to contrast it with the natural body. He is making the point that Christ's body after the Resurrection (and ours too) has different characteristics to it than it did before. There were some things that were different about it. And there will be some things that will be different about ours compared to what they are now. But the point is made very clearly that what is being talked about is the *same body*, the contrast here is not between physical body and spiritual body, but rather between the same body in different states or with different characteristics. Verse 44 is especially clear about the fact that it is the same body.

HABERMAS: Read verse 44.

BECK: Verse 44 says, "It is sown a physical body, it is raised a spiritual body." It is the same "it." And that is clear all the way through, that it is the same body. So now I have got a problem. First of all, in the context of what was being said last night, I think Gary needs to clarify and define carefully what he means by *spiritual body.* Tony, your constant prodding on that point was never quite answered and you were correct at that point. But I think once we get it clarified, it leaves your hypothesis, Tony, about a vision here, unacceptable in the light of what Paul is saying.

HABERMAS: If by *vision* we mean something that is subjective with no objective referent.

FLEW: I suppose we ought to make the familiar distinction between two senses of experience. In everyday experience, if I claim to have had experience with cows, I am claiming to have had actual dealings with them. In the philosophical sense, dreams of cows count as experience, because in the philosophical sense of the word *experience,* the claim to have had experience of X does not entail the claim that there was some mind-independent X there. Now I am allowing that Paul had an experience in the philosophical sense, which he interpreted as being an experience in everyday sense. Paul was taking it that there was a normally invisible object that he was actually experiencing in the everyday sense of experience.

MIETHE: Gary, define *spiritual body.*

HABERMAS: I thought we made a start when you read verse 44.

BECK: No, I want *you* to define what you are talking about.

HABERMAS: Okay. I would define a spiritual body in Paul's sense as a real body, the same body, but changed. Last night I said something like this: the Gospels and Paul teach similarly. We sometimes hear that the Gospels teach a flesh and blood body, and Paul teaches a spiritual body, and that there is a great difference there. As I said last night, the Gospels also show that Jesus' corporeal, post-Resurrection body also had different properties in the sense of going through the rock of the tomb, because when the stone was rolled away, he was already gone. He also went through closed doors. In the account of the trip to Emmaus in Luke 24, he is eating dinner with two followers one moment and disappears the next moment. So the Gospels by no means claim that Jesus' body was exactly the same as before or that it had exactly the same properties as before. No one had to open doors or the tomb in order for Jesus to get out. That is not the claim of the disciples. I would define Paul's usage similarly; I would argue for the Resurrection of the body. What is raised is the same body, and it is a real body, yet it is changed.

BECK: It seems clear that Paul is in fact talking about having literally seen, in sense data terms, a physical body, that he was not in any way referring to some kind of vision. The Greek is very clear, it uses the word *horaō*. It is clear that Paul is using ordinary observation terms and that he is referring to a physical body. An ordinary, plain, old body. It just is not clear to me why Paul should use that kind of language if Paul thought he had in fact seen a vision of something.

HABERMAS: Yes, Paul uses the same word that Luke does.

FLEW: Well, he thought he was seeing a spiritual body. I take it that a spiritual body is thought to be something that does not have ordinary, everyday characteristics of visibility and tangibility.

HABERMAS: That is a *spirit*. Paul says it is a spiritual *body*.

FLEW: Yes, I know. I think he's thinking in astral body terms. There are lots of people who have thought this sort of thing.

HABERMAS: Tertullian.

FLEW: Yes, a long tradition of thinking this sort of thing about there being spiritual bodies that are not normally visible but are really there just as much as any other thing. Yes, Tertullian is one example. I am not sure that he is exactly the same, but that sort of thing.

MIETHE: This may be an interpretation that people have made, but it is not based on any of the grammar, the wording, or the claims of the actual linguistics of the New Testament text.

FLEW: Yes, but to use the word *see* without quotes around it is going to be entirely correct if there really are the sorts of things that St. Paul is suggesting and you have the privilege of seeing.

MIETHE: But the point is that there is no reason to assume Paul is using the word *see* with quotes in an abnormal sense, because the Greek word for *body* is there. The Greek word that Luke uses for physical bodies is there. It is clearly, as Dave pointed out earlier, a contrast made not between different entities but a change in the same entity.

FLEW: You think of this as being a change in the same thing.

MIETHE: My point is that from the grammar, from the language in the New Testament text, there is no reason to assume anything different.

FLEW: Indeed, a perfectly normal usage of the word *to see,* especially the distinction between actually seeing, as with all words of perception, and seeing only in quotes. It is a distinction not about the experience, but about whether there is something actually there that you are acquiring information about. Paul thought he was actually acquiring information about something.

MIETHE: Something that was actually there.

FLEW: Yes, certainly.

HABERMAS: What was it that Paul experienced, a hallucination?

FLEW: I take it that there was not anything actually there that could be seen by anyone else in normal circumstances without a special gift.

MIETHE: Fine, except you have just admitted that you agree that St. Paul thought, and intended to say, that he saw something he thought was actually *there.*

FLEW: Oh yes, but he thought he saw a spiritual body.

MIETHE: Yes, body.

FLEW: But this whole thing about this notion of spiritual bodies, the people who believe in this sort of notion believe that these things are actually there but are not normally visible, not normally tangible, not normally sensible.

MIETHE: You are slipping into the assumption again that it is an astral body in some way.

FLEW: I am offering this as an explanation of the sort of thing that I take it that St. Paul meant. I am trying, sympathetically, to understand what a man, who is talking about the sorts of things that I do not normally spend time on, meant.

MIETHE: A moment ago, it seemed to me that we were getting something clear and now we have backed off from it again. You have admitted that Paul thought he was seeing a physical body, the same body of Jesus, but it was changed. But you think that he meant by that an astral body.

FLEW: Of course Paul thought he was seeing something that was proper to describe as the risen Lord. I also think that Paul thought that it was actual seeing in the sense that Paul believed he was in contact with a mind-independent reality. You asked me how he came to believe these things. I think what he had was a visionary experience and there was not anything there.

I feel that this is a straightforward interpretation, because Paul himself would not have thought that there was anything there that was accessible to any normal observation. But Paul has various beliefs about the universe that make it reasonable for him to interpret this vision in this way, so then we are not disagreeing about what is immediately observable. I do not think that St. Paul would have been put out if there had been anyone there at the time who said, "Well, we did not see anything." He thinks it was a rather special thing, doesn't he? He is not saying that, "Good heavens, the risen Lord landed on the road to Damascus available for everyone who happened to be passing by." The risen Lord made a special appearance to St. Paul.

13704

BECK: But the real point of Paul's use of the creed in 1 Corinthians 15 is just the fact that he was convinced that what he saw was exactly what all of these other people had also seen.

FLEW: Yes.

BECK: At this point we must go to the others as well. So far in the debate you, Tony, have simply dismissed all of the other evidence. I think we are going to have to come back to that, so I am going to start by asking Gary to state a case that we can bounce off of in terms of the reliability of the other witnesses whom Paul in part cites, and certainly in church history we have always cited.

HABERMAS: After I say two brief things about this other discussion I will try to answer your question. In verse 44 of 1 Corinthians 15, Paul says, speaking of the spiritual body, "It is sown a physical body, it is raised a spiritual body. If there is a physical body, there is also a spiritual body." Three times in that one verse the word *soma,* or "body," is used. I think what Terry and Dave have been trying to get to in the questions is that Paul does not say that the Resurrection body is a spirit. He says that there is a spiritual *soma* and there is a natural *soma*. We do injustice to Paul if we just ignore the word *soma* and stress the word *spiritual*. As scholars have pointed out, we must remember that there are two words in Paul's phrase: *spiritual* and *body*. Some people stress *body* too much; they do not get the *spiritual* in it. Others stress *spiritual* too much; they do not get the *body*. It has got to be both *spiritual* and *body*.

And you, Tony, said that Paul was not saying that anybody who was there with him on the road to Damascus could have seen Jesus. Again, as I said last night to you, I think you are going to have to make use of the texts in Acts 9, 22, and 26 here, because that is where the appearance to Paul is described in any detail. The text relates that the men traveling with Paul saw a light and heard the sound of the words that were spoken to Paul, but they did not understand them. But notice that the men with Paul did not simply stand and wonder why Paul stopped in the middle of the road.

But to get to Dave's question, how are we going to get back to the twelve? I do not think Paul was the subject of hallucinations, but having said that, neither do I base my entire case on Paul. Let us go back to the creed for a minute, because I still do not think this point has been answered. Let me just talk about those three verses in 1 Corinthians 15:3–5, because it is agreed by virtually all scholars that the creed includes at least verses 3, 4, and 5. The creed is reported by Paul, given to him by eyewitnesses, and that was based on experiences that occurred before they reported it to Paul. Who gave it to him? The eyewitnesses. And what does verse 5 report? It includes an appearance to Peter and a collective appearance to the disciples. How do we account for visions to eleven people if hallucinations cannot explain an appearance to such a group? I read the quote from a psychologist last night and today, and a hallucination to twelve people does not work. Twelve people do not see the same hallucination, nor can you induce hallucinations in other people.

BECK: Yes, but that was not my question. My question involved the fact that now we need to turn to the Gospels.

HABERMAS: Well, then, I will just say for the record that I do not think we have come to grips with the fact that 1 Corinthians 15:5 reports a collective appearance to the twelve. That is eyewitness testimony, and that cannot be accounted for by hallucinations. Now we will go to the Gospels.

FLEW: But I do not believe we have got sufficient reason to think that it happened at all.

HABERMAS: Well, it is reported by the people who were there. And naturalistic theories do not work.

FLEW: What we have in 1 Corinthians is St. Paul's statement that there was this experience happening to a dozen people. We have also got other evidence that St. Paul talked with one or two of the people in question. Oh, good heavens, would you hang a person on this evidence? You are wanting to transform your whole world on the basis of evidence that would never get a conviction. Any American court with a decent defense lawyer would throw this out. It is evidence for the prosecution. If you had two chaps reporting that they and another ten fellows had killed a man, and you had another chap saying that he had met these two fellows, and they had reported that they had gotten together with another ten chaps and committed a murder, what American judge would accept that, saying, "Well, we have got to hang the men who committed the murder. We have the evidence of twelve people, and they have confessed to this murder."

MIETHE: You could hang the men on two other very important things: one is checking out the claim that Paul also says that these other twelve were also concurrently preaching the same facts at the same time. You could put the twelve on the witness stand. That could be checked out. And two, as I pointed out last night and it was never addressed, the claims of seeing Jesus' resurrected body are close enough in time to the original event that we have dozens, dozens of eyewitnesses running around, the church is causing all this havoc, the Roman empire is being affected, so much so that Caesar's household is involved, and Christians are being persecuted, very soon after these events. Why did not someone simply put a stop to it by disproving the claims?

FLEW: Well, what are these people supposed to do? What is the date of the operation? You are not referring to the Neronian persecution, are you?

MIETHE: No, I am talking about the apostles, the movements, the claims in Acts that the Jewish leaders were trying to suppress the message, but were not successful.

FLEW: Yes, well, again we have got no independent evidence of this early attempt to suppress it, have we? We have got no detailed stuff about that.

MIETHE: Except that it makes sense. Why not do it anyway? Why not have the Jews do it anyway?

FLEW: How is this going to be? What are they supposed to do? They are presumably supposed to get hold of one or two of these apostles and try to get them to testify that they never had any experiences at all or they did not have it as a group. Suppose they do this in Jerusalem and get this done? Does it get all around the world?

MIETHE: They do not have to get it all around the world, just a very small province where claims are being made and where historical records of the other side would exist somewhere to say, "Look, it was clearly shown, the claims are false, other independent sources checked out the evidence and though perhaps the apostles, disciples, early Christians refused to accept the evidence, there is clearly evidence to the contrary." In other words, I am saying that there were astute people around in that day who would have asked for the same kind of evidence for the claims of Christianity and would have taken it as a moral duty to have written down for posterity falsifications of the claims.

FLEW: I do not think this is true at all. All this is assuming that the young Christian movement was recognized as the important thing it was going to become. But it was not, after all, there is virtually no non-Christian evidence about anything in the Christian movement in the early years. It begins to turn up, we get the reference in Josephus, which scholars consider a corruption of the text, and we get some other accurate things in Josephus, which indicate that he does not believe, and we get Pliny's letter, other things like that later on. Then lots and lots of evidence from outside. But for the crucial first period, there is nothing.

MIETHE: A corrupt thing that says Josephus does not believe it, but he has obviously heard it and it must have been heard by others.

FLEW: Oh yes, Josephus has heard something about it, but clearly it does not appear as a very big matter to Josephus. This is interesting to ask because of what happened afterward, but it clearly was not a big thing. You cannot think that they were all mad keen to suppress it.

MIETHE: No, but if Josephus had in fact heard about it, there was enough of something going on that some people surely would have taken it upon themselves to verify it independently of the claims of the disciples.

FLEW: I doubt if you can assume that this would be going on. I suppose the way to get some sort of varied cross-check on this is to see how much evidence of a discrediting character we have about the origins of other religious movements in that period. Is anything known about it?

HABERMAS: Oh yes, let's talk about it.

BECK: What is amazing is that so far we have said almost nothing about the four Gospels. So far you have sort of dismissed the four Gospels out of hand, Tony, and I guess I want to know apart from allegations you, Tony, made about inconsistencies and that sort of thing, why should you do that? On what basis are you rejecting the fairly consistent claims that at least two of these Gospels are written by eyewitnesses and that the other two are authorized by eyewitnesses and used by them in the proclamation of their Gospels?

FLEW: Well, I have latched on to St. Paul because this was the earliest statement made by someone about a Resurrection appearance directly after the event. There is a big difference, even as to eyewitness testimony, between that which is made shortly after the event and that made a long time after, when the eyewitnesses have had a lot of time to think about it, reinterpret it, and wonder about its significance.

BECK: But that is not generally true in court. A case can come up twenty or thirty years later, and if the eyewitnesses can still corroborate their testimony it is as good as that made the day after. I do not see what a long time here has to do with anything.

FLEW: Why I brought in parapsychology was that it did seem to me to be the nearest secular analogy to this investigation of the miraculous. Because here one is dealing with investigation into things that one has a lot of reason to believe are impossible.

BECK: That would only be true given your account of what Paul meant by *spiritual body*. Given any other account it has no parallel at all with parapsychology.

FLEW: On the contrary, if I am right about Paul, there is nothing impossible at all about what I attribute to Paul. What makes it analogous to parapsychology is *your* claims about the whole affair. That there was a supreme miracle that occurred and that certain appearances and experiences are evidence for the occurrence of the miracle. Now when you are dealing with that, you need carefully examined testimony for it. We have the extra complication that we are dealing with claims in which the Gospel writers are seeing something that they attribute to the ministry of Jesus as a fulfillment of prophecy, where it is clear that the story was shaped by prophecy.

MIETHE: Why do you dismiss the two Gospels that claim to be eyewitness accounts and the two that claim to be authorized by eyewitnesses? Simply because they were written twenty years later?

FLEW: I am not dismissing them out of hand on every ground, but all these factors have greatly weakened the value of their testimony when it is testimonies of the miraculous.

MIETHE: An analogy is often made to Franklin D. Roosevelt (though it is not quite the same thing). Claims are made about him forty years after his death. He is not around. Can't those claims be checked out?

FLEW: Yes. Of course.

MIETHE: Why weren't they in Jesus' case? It seems to me that you are caught in the position of denying the veracity of the claims while there were plenty of eyewitnesses around so that the evidence could be checked out. We do not have to talk about the A.D. first century. We do not have to talk about after John dies or when Augustine comes on the scene. We have enough information, building of the church, impact of the church, things going on by way of reactions within the first twenty years or so that the claims could be checked out. This is Dave's point. Just because we are removed twenty years from the events of the Gospels, you cannot automatically label it a parapsychology experience, can you?

FLEW: Regarding some things, the things we are talking about, yes. Other things in there could be checked if you could find someone who was a witness of that thing. Let us take one event that could have been easily checked out by anyone who was in Jerusalem at the time—the earthquake in Matthew or the rending of the veil of the temple, say, or the other sort of opening of the tombs that was occurring—all of these things could be checked out, yes indeed, they could. But why, if they actually occurred, are they not mentioned in the other Gospels?

BECK: But they are mentioned in other sources.

FLEW: What other sources? Other sources prior to Matthew?

BECK: Yes, prior to Matthew, and mentioned by other historians. Not the earthquake itself, but the darkness and the events surrounding the Crucifixion.

FLEW: By whom?

BECK: By Thallus, whose words are recorded by Julius Africanus.

HABERMAS: Yes, Thallus mentioned it about A.D. 52.

FLEW: Really.

HABERMAS: That is one of those eighteen extrabiblical sources I spoke of earlier.

FLEW: The more evidence you have for these sort of publicly available extraordinary events, the more difficulty you will have in explaining why it is that more people were not impressed by them.

HABERMAS: First of all, you are picking some occurrences in Matthew that are not reported in the other four Gospels, right? That is not the case for the Resurrection, because it is reported by all four Gospels, so this is a stronger claim. And there is eyewitness testimony behind the Gospels, as both the questioners have been stating here, so it is certainly not analogous to use an example where only one Gospel states something because, again, you have five chapters in four Gospels that mention the Resurrection. Let us also mention Acts 1, because that is the second volume of Luke. So we have six chapters that mention Jesus' Resurrection body. We cannot compare that to three verses about the veil being torn, tombs emptying, and people walking around.

FLEW: No, but the great thing about these other things is that they are accessible to everyone in Jerusalem and not things that were allegedly revealed to and accessible to only the small group of the followers of Jesus.

MIETHE: How is it that the Resurrection was not accessible to everyone in Jerusalem?

FLEW: What is accessible to them is that the followers of Jesus are claiming that they have seen the resurrected Jesus.

MIETHE: But it was not only the followers of Jesus who saw Jesus. And the occurrences went on for forty days.

HABERMAS: For instance, we have at least two people, James and Paul, who were not believers before they saw the resurrected Jesus: James's unbelief is recorded in the Gospels (but compare 1 Corinthians 15:7) and Paul later, of course. So Jesus did not appear only to "prejudiced" witnesses; he also appeared to enemies.

FLEW: Yes, but this is a completely different case. I mean, you are wanting to have these as cases where either it is claimed that a lot of people saw it simultaneously, so it cannot have been a collective hallucination, or cases such as the Thomas case, where it is much more than a vision, where the body is touched.

HABERMAS: But a key point here is that we have four Gospels. With Mark, we could debate whether there's anything beyond 16:8, but in the other three Gospels, Matthew, Luke, and John, Jesus either offers to be touched or is touched. There are eyewitness sources behind the Gospels and they are only one generation after the creed and after the Crucifixion, so we have got to account for that.

FLEW: Got to. You may not be able to account for it, though. And it is a terribly long time after this. Again, if you think of this from the point of view of someone wanting to put out a revelation, it is an extraordinary way of going about it. Surely anyone who wants to prove anything in this world tries to provide bags of evidence, bags of verification. Here we have to piece together a few things. Absolutely nothing from any non-Christian source at the time.

HABERMAS: Well, Thallus.

FLEW: If any person were having a revelation in the modern world and were having it under a colonial regime somewhere, surely they would take care that it was entered into the records of the authorities. Here these earth-shattering events were supposed to have occurred in Jerusalem, and all you have is years after the events simply a testimony from one or two followers as to what happened years and years ago, with claims about how you could have asked unspecified people who are scattered all over the eastern world about these events. Extraordinary, is it not?

HABERMAS: Let me go back to an earlier question from Tony. Could these disciples have been put on the witness stand? That is a key question. All we have got is Paul, you said, because the Gospels are too late. Could the twelve disciples be put on the witness stand (or eleven plus Matthias)? How could they have been put on the witness stand? To repeat my arguments, which I think still need to be answered: First, I Corinthians 15:5 is an early, eyewitness report of a collective appearance that still must be explained. Tony keeps saying that this is not good enough evidence. Not only do we have more than these two eyewitnesses (Peter and James) plus Paul, however, as I will point out in a moment, but I want to note that simply scoffing at the evidence is not the same as answering it adequately. These two eyewitnesses to collective appearances have not been disproven.

Number two, in I Corinthians 15:11 and 14–15 Paul states that the disciples were also teaching that Jesus appeared to them. This is a report concerning the eyewitnesses and this second case includes more than two. And since Paul (in Gal. 2:1–10; cf. 1:18–20) reports personal contact with the original disciples for the specific purpose of checking the content of the Gospel, which includes the resurrection (I Cor. 15:3–4), it is not very likely that Paul was mistaken in this claim concerning Jesus' collective appearances.

Number three, there is eyewitness testimony behind the Gospels. Let us go back to something I said last night in the debate. Your professor, Tony, at Oxford, A. N. Sherwin-White, went on record as saying that Luke is a good historian, and in one passage in *Roman Society and Roman Law in the New Testament,* Sherwin-White says that Luke's record has long been accepted by Roman historians as an excellent source even in the details. And not only Acts but the Gospels also are said to be trustworthy historical sources for the life of Jesus. These books do not pervert the major historical facts. As Sherwin-White also points out, the Gospels are much closer to the facts that they report than is much of accepted Roman history. Some hold that Roman history is different from the Gospels, with the latter being largely religious mythology, but this is also denied.[6]

Let me also add here the work of Sir William Ramsay, the archaeologist, who said the same about Acts.[7] But Sherwin-White is more recent, as well as a world-renowned Roman authority, and he says that the Book of Acts is an excellent source. Acts starts out in the first eleven verses by recording the Resurrection appearances and the Ascension. Acts 1:3, from the same book that Sherwin-White says is such an excellent source even in the details, states that "To them he presented himself alive after his passion by many proofs. . . ." Just two verses before that, in Acts 1:1, Luke starts out by saying that this is volume two, which follows the first volume, which was also written to Theophilus (the Gospel of Luke). The same man who wrote Acts also wrote the Book of Luke, and in Luke 24 we have an account of the resurrected Jesus. To tie this all together, the word *horaō*, "seen," is used by both Paul in 1 Corinthians 15 and by Luke in Luke 24. The disciples saw the risen Jesus and, as you noted, Jesus offered to be touched in Luke 24.

So these are three arguments that still must be answered: (1) The creed states that the disciples collectively saw Jesus in verse 5, so hallucinations do not work. (2) Paul said that the same disciples were preaching about the Resurrection appearances to them, so you could have placed them on the witness stand. And although you say that we do not have good testimony, we certainly do; that is what the creed is, the creed is their eyewitness testimony, plus the same men were still preaching it. (3) The Gospels are trustworthy sources. Someone such as A. N. Sherwin-White says that the Gospels are fine historical sources for Jesus. I think these are three strong arguments that say that the eyewitnesses could be placed on the stand and that their testimony would be vindicated.

FLEW: Well, Luke is one thing. Acts is another. And although I will not dispute anything that my respected old tutor at Oxford said, a book can be a very good source about the acts of the Apostles without being any sort of account of what was going on in Jerusalem in roughly A.D. 30. That is the crucial thing here. Acts is clearly the very best thing we have got about the early church.

MIETHE: Why assume that Luke and Acts are of different qualities? The testimony of scholars throughout the history of the world since these events has been that when we check out Luke and Acts we find them to be reliable, historical accounts of what was happening politically, about the methods of travel, about the time it took to travel from place to place, and so forth. Why then assume that we can immediately rule them out when they talk about something "spiritual"? Why assume that Luke and Acts are no longer reliable?

FLEW: Well, we raise our eyebrows when he starts recording events that are not so much improbable as naturally impossible. It is at that stage we should demand evidence of a much higher order than we demand when it is an everyday event. That is the point at which the situation changes. And this, of course, is what everyone would consider if it was not this case in which many people believe this was a special revelation case. You find recorded somewhere in Augustine's works a couple of resurrections, and no one has treated those accounts seriously.

BECK: I still have not gotten an answer as to why we have to reject the Gospels as being eyewitness or secondhand reports of eyewitnesses.

FLEW: Okay, one or two of them may be written by people who were in Jerusalem at the time. They were written a long time afterward, though, and there was a great deal of time for rethinking and reconsideration. After all, there are many differences just between the Gospels.

BECK: But that does not hurt. And I do not see why ten to twenty years is a long time. You had no problem this afternoon recounting events that were more than ten or twenty years ago.

FLEW: Yes, but not this sort of event. Oh, no.

BECK: I do not see why "this sort of event" has anything to do with the time factor.

FLEW: What is a long time in one context is not a long time in another context.

HABERMAS: The Gospels are outdated at thirty to sixty years after the Cross? A. N. Sherwin-White has already laid this charge to rest, as have other scholars. The Gospels, when judged by the standards of ancient historical writing, are very good historical sources. So thirty to sixty years is not too long to preclude good historical writing. And renowned historians and archaeologists have found these books to be accurate. Remember I asked you last night in the debate why do we not mention Plato when there are one thousand to fifteen hundred years between some of his works and some of the earliest copies?

FLEW: There is no reason to dispute Plato, of course, because he makes no claims as to this kind of event.

MIETHE: I wonder how we will get to the logic of the point that is continually being made here. Doesn't it seem like we are almost saying: "Because we do not like the implications of the claims of this event, twenty years between the event and the report suddenly becomes such a long time that we cannot accept it." This was my point about the historical accuracy of Luke and Acts. You say we need much better evidence, but the point is that scholars (Ramsay and many others) say that we have highly accurate statements about everything else in Luke and Acts. Yet you, Tony, jump to the claim that this is not good enough evidence any more.

FLEW: No, it is not that we do not like this, we may like it or may not like it at all. It is that we have the best of reasons for thinking that this is naturally impossible. One of the things we went through last night in the debate was that none of the parties to this debate can afford to weaken the claims that we would ordinarily make about natural possibility and natural impossibility. If you are going to say there is nothing particularly remarkable and out-of-the-way about a resurrection, then the whole value of this as a validation disappears.

MIETHE: Obviously we are not wanting to say that (or willing to say that), but the question becomes what sort of evidence would be good enough, then, to accept the claims to a Resurrection?

FLEW: An awful lot would be required. If you had very good reasons for expecting a revelation, that would be the sort of thing that would swing it, because it would provide a reason for abandoning the ordinary assumptions of naturalistic history.

BECK: It is still not clear to me why ten to twenty years is a long time, but in any case, the written Gospel was not the first time someone said something about the Resurrection. The claims about the Resurrection start popping up almost immediately.

FLEW: Oh certainly, yes. They do start popping up immediately.

BECK: Okay, so I do not even have ten to twenty years.

FLEW: Ah, but what is happening is that there become different sorts of claims.

BECK: No, they do not seem to be. That is just the point of tracing down the creed; the evidence is clear that from the very beginning, immediately after the event all the way up to the writing of the Gospels, the claims are identical. There is no difference. There is no development.

FLEW: The claim is being made that there were Resurrection appearances. That is what they are saying.

HABERMAS: Who claimed that?

BECK: The claims are being made by eyewitnesses, who claim that they saw a body, a physical body, that had been dead three days previously and had come back.

HABERMAS: Tony, did the original eyewitnesses claim to have seen the risen Jesus?

FLEW: Well, that is what St. Paul was claiming, wasn't it?

HABERMAS: Okay. But what about the disciples. Did they claim this too?

FLEW: Who knows what they claimed at the time? I suppose they claimed something of this sort, yes. I would expect it.

HABERMAS: They did. Finally! Then how do you explain twelve people seeing a vision if hallucinations do not work?

BECK: And a lot more than twelve.

FLEW: But there is a world of difference between admitting that the people who originally claimed to have seen the Resurrection believed this and saying that twelve people claimed to have seen it together.

HABERMAS: That is contained in the creed, though. You still must do away with the creed, and verse 5 in particular, where the collective appearance to eyewitnesses is reported.

FLEW: That is what somebody else is saying happened.

HABERMAS: No, that is what the disciples themselves said.

BECK: But even if they did not see it together, a lot of people on different occasions at different times saw the same thing, and hallucinations will not explain that.

FLEW: Oh, but it will explain that if they were seeing it on different occasions.

BECK: I do not think you are even going to get that. Hallucinations are not going to account for that many people on that many different occasions in groups of two, three, four, whatever seeing the same thing.

FLEW: Wait a minute, the number of people seeing this separately is not an issue. There is a world of difference between twelve people seeing it together and twelve people seeing it on separate occasions.

BECK: Even if two people on separate occasions saw *this* kind of same thing, I would find that utterly astounding.

FLEW: But the number of people who have had visions of Shiva, for example, is enormous.

HABERMAS: One at a time, or twelve at a time?

FLEW: One at a time, yes.

HABERMAS: But that is not the case with the Resurrection appearances. And even if we have claims in other religions concerning visions witnessed by more than one person at a time, these claims must be checked for the chance of legend and the likelihood of false reporting or other possibilities, just like we did with the Resurrection.

FLEW: You and Dave are doing different things here.

MIETHE: That is true.

FLEW: Dave keeps saying that it is the mere number of people who have claimed the vision and Gary is wanting to insist, very properly, that what makes the difference evidentially is that a lot of people are seeing it at the same time. I think there is a world of difference.

BECK: I think both points are valid.

HABERMAS: I do not think we are contradicting each other.

MIETHE: Tony, do we have a group of eyewitnesses who claim to have seen Jesus?

FLEW: Well, there is a difference between an eyewitness who claims that a group of people saw Jesus and a group of eyewitnesses claiming that together they saw Jesus. And what we have, possibly, is eyewitnesses claiming that a group of people saw Jesus. What we do not have is the group of people who claimed they saw it together who are all, of course, eyewitnesses of this one thing together (or claiming to be), and there they were producing this collective statement.

HABERMAS: Numerous critical scholars have attested that one of the strongest facts in early Christian history is that the earliest disciples, the original eyewitnesses, believed that the resurrected Jesus appeared to them. First of all, Rudolf Bultmann states in "New Testament and Mythology," page 42, in the Harper & Row edition: "All that historical criticism can establish is the fact that the first disciples came to believe in the resurrection." So even Bultmann holds that history can establish this fact.[8] German historian Hans Von Campenhausen asserts concerning the creed in 1 Corinthians 15:3 ff. that "This account meets all the demands of historical reliability that could possibly be made of such a text."[9] British New Testament scholar A. M. Hunter states that "The passage therefore preserves uniquely early and verifiable testimony. It meets every reasonable demand of historical reliability."[10] And last, Michael Grant, in his book *Jesus: An Historian's Review of the Gospels*, points out on page 176 that history can "prove" that the earliest eyewitnesses believed that Jesus appeared to them.[11]

Tony just raised a good point, the question being that if some people saw the resurrected Jesus, that is not the same as a group of people seeing him. But Bultmann, Von Campenhausen, Hunter, and Grant all say that the earliest disciples claimed to have seen the resurrected Jesus. Even Bultmann speaks of group appearances to the disciples.[12] Now I would go to the creed and to the Gospels, which say that the twelve collectively saw Jesus.

1 Corinthians 15:5 is eyewitness testimony, which says that the eleven saw Jesus together, the Gospels say the same thing, and Paul says that the original disciples were proclaiming it at the same time. These are the same three facts that I raised earlier. Tony has just said that we do not have eyewitnesses who say that they saw Jesus collectively, but all three of these categories present just such evidence. (1) Peter and James not only reported the creed, but they were, respectively, part of the groups mentioned in 1 Corinthians 15:5 and 7 that personally saw the risen Jesus. Here we must remember that the creed is not Pauline; it is not Paul's, but the report of the eyewitnesses themselves. This is crucial. To say that we do not have reports from the actual group members, but only Paul's word, is to deny this last point. (2) To the extent to which we have eyewitness testimony in the Gospels we have further and independent eyewitness reports of the resurrected Jesus. Remember the earlier testimony of scholars such as Sherwin-White and Dodd on this point. (3) Last, unless Paul is completely mistaken in spite of his excellent position from which to know, the original disciples were preaching about their experiences with the risen Jesus, including the collective appearances. What makes Paul's testimony even more valuable is the fact that he had several interviews with the eyewitnesses. Again, the Gospel (which includes the Resurrection as a central tenet

—1 Corinthians 15:1–3) was the major topic in these discussions (Acts 15; Galatians 1:18–20 and 2:1–10). Even critical scholars will grant this, and Von Campenhausen and Hunter have even asserted that this evidence is historically reliable. Thus the eyewitness testimony could be cross-examined and would excel on the witness stand. Unless you are prepared to say, Tony, that eleven people and other groups can see hallucinations, I think your hypothesis is in trouble here.

MIETHE: All right, this raises the very question I have been trying to raise for the past half hour. You have stated repeatedly, Gary, that you have a core facts argument, and that this core facts argument is accepted by numerous historians of international reputation in history (unquestionably critics of a fundamentalist or an evangelical position), who say the textual claims of the New Testament support the Resurrection. Tony disagrees. What is it about the core facts, or the quality of the evidence, that makes these internationally recognized historians, almost all of them critics, admit those facts? What about the facts is so strong that they have to accept them?

HABERMAS: It depends on which critics you are talking about, but many scholars are convinced largely because of the evidence from the creed. Critics on the far left, the further left they go, the less they are going to trust the Gospels. They are going to side with Tony, Bultmann, and so on. But no matter how far left they go, those who believe that the earliest eyewitnesses claimed to have seen the risen Jesus (which is virtually everyone, even in this group) generally recognize the importance of the creed in 1 Corinthians 15. Then you move toward the middle, toward the more moderate critics, mostly the British scholars such as C. H. Dodd, A. M. Hunter, and others, even John A. T. Robinson toward the end of his life. They often argue, as does Dodd, for instance, that there are historical passages in the Gospels that are early and reflect eyewitness testimony about the risen Jesus. As you get a little closer to the generally conservative view, they put more emphasis on the eyewitness testimony behind the Gospels, and that becomes a third resource for evidence. So no matter how far left one goes and no matter how critical one gets, the fact is that virtually all of these scholars recognize that the eyewitnesses at least believed that they saw the risen Jesus. The creed is crucial here—it may be called the minimum facts accepted by scholars. And since it is realized that naturalistic theories do not provide a factual alternative, we are left with the eyewitness testimony which has convinced so many to accept the literal Resurrection. Plus we still have the witness of the Gospels and Paul's testimony concerning the disciples also teaching about their Resurrection appearances.

MIETHE: Let us take John A. T. Robinson, for instance. What moved him from his position earlier in life, obviously a stance that would be much closer to Tony's position, about the critical nature of the text to a position with statements that astounded the scholarly world by his saying that the texts of the New Testament were so reliable?

HABERMAS: In one of Robinson's earlier works, *Exploration into God,* he notes that although he finds the miraculous virgin birth easier to whisk away, the facts for the empty tomb are not that easy to ignore.[13] We have that even in *Exploration into God.* But in one of his later books, *Can We Trust the New Testament?,* he includes a section about ten pages long on the Resurrection. He argues that the Resurrection creed in 1 Corinthians 15 is very early and provides some strong evidence for the Resurrection. Also, Robinson notes that the naturalistic theories do not work. He even mentions the Shroud of Turin. This is not very well known, but John Robinson was probably the chief New Testament scholar to work with the scientists in the pre-1978 studies, and he published two proshroud articles. One appears in a collected set of essays by my coauthor, Ken Stevenson.[14] So in those ten pages he mentions the early creed and the failure of the naturalistic theories and some evidence for the Resurrection. You will have to go to his other articles to get his material on the Shroud of Turin. By the way, in that same book Robinson also argues that there is eyewitness testimony behind the Gospels and that they are trustworthy sources. I think he believed that some literal and objective experiences occurred to the disciples. He specifically notes that the experiences were not subjective.

MIETHE: Yes, but there is a whole book that says now we can trust the New Testament and before we could not.

HABERMAS: That is right.

BECK: Tony has yet to make any reference to the shroud.

FLEW: Well, I do not know anything about the shroud. I think the evidential questions are in a way interestingly different about this case. Oddly, this is a case where the testimonial evidence is entirely negative after you have the remarkable statement (admittedly secondhand, which is a weakness) of the bishop in control of the thing at about the first time it appears in the records, saying that it was all a fraud, carefully painted. This is a remarkable thing to happen; it is rather like the managing director of a highly competitive business announcing that its major product is not what it was claimed to be.

HABERMAS: Do you think it is a painting?

FLEW: I am just saying that this is what was said by the first bishop to make a record of the thing. This bishop was surely the successor of the bishop under which the thing first appeared. Isn't that right?

HABERMAS: Yes, you are right. Let me see if I understand your objection. Because the local medieval bishop claimed that the shroud was a cleverly painted object, this is a damaging criticism of the shroud. The man on the scene of the crime, so to speak, said that it was a painting.

FLEW: Well, no. This is a very remarkable, very odd thing. Now I have not said anything about the actual investigation of the shroud. This would start me off with a suspicion about it, but I would start off with a suspicion anyway.

BECK: Why don't we get the full answer before we go on.

FLEW: Clearly this person, like everyone else, can be wrong about this. Well, anyway, presumably it could be shown that there were no ordinary pigments in the stuff. Carbon-dating would be a good way of decisively falsifying the claims of the shroud.

HABERMAS: Let me take your comments in reverse. I will agree with you that if the shroud can be legitimately carbon-dated, and it is not first century, that is going to have to be faced by anybody who says the shroud is authentic. I will grant you that. I will note a problem with carbon-dating, however. Some publications raise the question of how accurately the shroud can be carbon-dated, because cloth is not like a stone or a piece of metal. It is difficult to carbon-date cloth exactly because it is so easily impregnated with foreign substances, and if it is not cleaned properly, one may improperly date the cloth. But it might be actually proved that the shroud is not a first-century object. Ken Stevenson and I have said in our book that the shroud could be a fake.

But to turn to your question concerning the medieval bishop, D'Arcis, who said that the shroud was a painting, let us remember something important: there were a number of shrouds, perhaps dozens, floating around Europe in the Middle Ages. Now one major problem with the bishop's claim is that we do not know the shroud about which he was talking. In one of my slide presentations I have a picture of a painted shroud, and it is not the Shroud of Turin. The painted figure is rather grotesque, and usually when I put it on the screen, people just laugh at it. It looks like a first grader's drawing. So the bishop's statement does not necessarily apply to the Shroud of Turin.

Additionally, as you noted, Tony, there is a test of falsifiability. We do not have to know how somebody could have painted it, but science is adept at finding paint when it is present. But first, if the scientists have come up with one major conclusion, it is that the shroud is not a known fake. There is no paint, dye, powder, or other foreign substance on the image fibrils that could account for the image. Microchemical analyses revealed no paints or pigments. Also, fraud is refuted by the shroud's 3-D characteristics. Paintings do not produce a 3-D effect, but the shroud image is 3-D. This has been checked out in a laboratory. In addition, the shroud image is superficial, which means that it is only on the top few fibrils of the affected threads. Each thread has about 200 fibrils, and the image is on the top few fibrils only. It does not even soak to the back threads, let alone to the back of the cloth. Paint is not superficial, and reproducing the shroud has not been possible in the laboratory.

Further, there are no plateaus or saturation points on the shroud image. But if you apply any pigment or dye there will naturally be saturation points. Still further, the shroud image is nondirectional.

Now if one is going to put paint on a cloth, one moves the hand from side to side. When one gets tired, one often starts moving the hand up and down. But even if one only moves from side to side all of the time, that is directionality. One cannot generally apply paint without directionality. If one uses a spray gun it still involves directionality. But there is no directionality on the shroud image. Also, there is no capillary flow on the shroud, which rules out any liquid movement. In addition, the 1532 fire that the shroud was involved in would have caused chemical changes in organic pigments, but there are no changes in the shroud. Further, the water applied to the shroud to put out the 1532 fire would usually cause chemical changes, but there are no such changes observed on the shroud.[15]

Finally, the shroud image is nontraditional. For instance, the nail wounds are in the wrists and the crown of thorns appears to be a skullcap. Someone painting the shroud in the Middle Ages would presumably not have known that the nails were placed in the wrists. A 1982 report from a team of scientists, released at a New London, Connecticut, meeting, states that, "No pigments, paints, dyes or stains have been found in the fibrils."[16] So again, we could falsify the shroud if there was paint. But they have not found any. Now maybe they will find some in the future. I am open to that, but right now that is a weak hypothesis. I cannot speak for anybody on the team of scientists, but just judging from their publications, the fraud thesis is the one theory that, according to a recent survey, nobody on the team of scientists holds. I think I would even say that this would be the easiest theory to refute. The shroud image does not appear to be painted at all.

NOTES

1. Sherwin-White, *Roman Society and Roman Law in the New Testament* (Oxford: Oxford University Press, 1963; Grand Rapids, MI: Baker Books, 1978), 186, 190; Grant, *Jesus: An Historian's Review of the Gospels* (New York: Scribner, 1977), 184.
2. Collins, personal correspondence.
3. For examples, see Raymond E. Brown, *The Gospel According to John,* vol. 1 (Garden City, NY: Doubleday, 1966), 87–104; Hunter, *Jesus: Lord and Saviour* (Grand Rapids, MI: Eerdmans, 1976), "The Trustworthiness of the Gospels"; John A. T. Robinson,

Can We Trust the New Testament? (Grand Rapids, MI: Eerdmans, 1977); F. F. Bruce, *The New Testament Documents: Are They Reliable?* 5th ed. (Grand Rapids, MI: Eerdmans, 1960).

4. Jeremias, *The Eucharistic Words of Jesus,* trans. Norman Perrin (London: SCM Press, 1966), 101–103; Fuller, *The Formation of the Resurrection Narratives* (New York: Macmillan, 1971), 10–11.

5. Bultmann, *Theology of the New Testament,* trans. Kendrick Grobel (New York: Scribner, 1951, 1955), vol. I, 27, 50.

6. Sherwin-White, *Roman Society and Roman Law in the New Testament,* 186–193.

7. William Ramsay, *The Bearing of Recent Discovery on the Trustworthiness of the New Testament* (Grand Rapids, MI: Baker Book House, 1953), 81.

8. Bultmann, "New Testament and Mythology," in *Kerygma and Myth,* ed. Hans Werner Bartsch, revised trans. Reginald Fuller (New York: Harper & Row, 1961), 42.

9. Hans Von Campenhausen, "The Events of Easter and the Empty Tomb," in *Tradition and Life in the Church* (Philadelphia: Fortress Press, 1968), 44.

10. Hunter, *Jesus: Lord and Saviour,* 100.

11. Grant, *Jesus: An Historian's Review of the Gospels,* 176.

12. Bultmann, *Theology of the New Testament,* vol. I, 45.

13. John A. T. Robinson, *Exploration Into God* (Stanford, CA: Stanford University Press, 1967), 113.

14. ———, "The Shroud of Turin and the Grave Cloths of the Gospels," in Kenneth Stevenson, ed., *Proceedings of the 1977 United States Conference of Research on the Shroud of Turin* (Bronx: Holy Shroud Guild, 1977).

15. See Gary R. Habermas and Kenneth E. Stevenson, *Verdict on the Shroud* (Wayne, PA: Dell, 1981), 246–249.

16. STRP "Text," New London, CT, 1981, 1.

III. RESPONSE TO THE DEBATE

Wolfhart Pannenberg

When, twenty years ago, I published my article "Did Jesus Really Rise from the Dead?",[1] a year after the German version of my Christology book appeared, which discussed the issue at length, the reaction of theologians was one of bewilderment. For quite a time, few critical theologians had dared to take the Easter reports of the New Testament seriously as raising claims to the historicity of the reported event. The general opinion among theologians was that the disciples of Jesus and, later on, the Apostle Paul had visionary experiences, the rest being a matter of interpretation. Concerning the empty-tomb tradition, at least in Germany Bultmann's judgment that this story was a late Hellenistic legend was widely accepted. When in 1952 Hans von Campenhausen defended the historicity of the empty tomb,[2] he was virtually alone against the common sense of historical scholarship in biblical exegesis. But even von Campenhausen did not claim historicity for the Resurrection itself, because the reality of that event seemed to belong to a different category of reality altogether—the eschatological reality of a new immortal life—rather than anything occurring in human history. Therefore it seemed appropriate to admit that the reality of that event must be a matter of faith, not of historical reason. This view has continued to be very influential, and usually serves as an argument for rejecting the empty-tomb tradition too, because it saves the theologian from quarrels against the principles of secular historiography, while at the same time offering a pious reason for doing so.

This attitude is largely consonant with that of David Hume, who, as a matter of principle, rejected the possibility of miracles and especially, of a real resurrection of a dead person, as "most contrary to custom and experience."[3] But when Hume in his section on miracles made the ironic remark that "our most holy religion is founded on faith, not on reason" concerning its belief in miracles and especially in its basic belief in the Resurrection of Jesus, he did not mean that an act of faith could render such a miracle credible. On the contrary, he meant that such an assumption had to be rejected by any reasonable person. It is in vain to assume one could accept Hume's position as far as historical judgment goes and still claim that the Resurrection of Jesus occurred as an event but that because of its "eschatological" character cannot be called "historical." Rather, the real question is whether any event occurred at all, and if so, what kind of event. The rules of historical method have been designed to deal with questions such as this. Therefore, it is self-contradictory to claim the occurrence of an event while at the same time rejecting the competence of historical judgment in judging the facticity of that event. Conversely, to claim that an event happened at a particular time and place implies logically a claim to historicity. This kind of claim does not first arise with the employment of evidence to corroborate it. It is only the explicitly historical statement that takes the form of a judgment based on evidence. But prior to it, any assertion concerning the past by implication raises a claim to historicity, and this is precisely the fact that calls for discriminatory historical judgment. In this sense the Christian message that Jesus was raised from the dead inevitably implies a claim to historicity, because it is meant that this happened at a certain time and place. And if in the course of a critical discussion of the Easter tradition one arrives at the conclusion that there are sufficiently good reasons to continue with that claim and message, then such a conclusion involves an explicitly historical judgment. Therefore, during the past twenty years, I have argued that Christian theology cannot avoid taking a stand concerning the historicity of Jesus' Resurrection. To say this does not necessarily presuppose an overly optimistic assessment of the evidence, but it is a logical requirement for talking about Jesus as risen and for accounting for such language.

In recent years the prejudices preventing the modesty and soberness of a rational discussion of this issue seem to have lessened. In this respect the discussion between Antony Flew and Gary Habermas is encouraging. The first important step of progress is that Professor Flew, although he argues in the line of Hume's position, explicitly acknowledges that what I earlier called the dogmatism in Hume's position is no longer supportable: an a priori rejection of the possibility of miracles cannot be justified. This point was made very well by Professor Habermas in his first response to Flew's paper and, especially in the question and answer period, Professor Flew explicitly agreed to this point. This means that whether an asserted event is to be accepted as historical finally has to be a matter of the evidence. Professor Flew, of course, is correct in his contention (which is the main point he shares with Hume) that the amount of evidence needed to convince us that something very unusual or exceptional has happened is considerably larger than in the case of familiar sequences of events. It also must be admitted that the plausibility structure of historical reconstruction is to be based on customary rules of regular occurrences unless it becomes apparent that in particular cases such an assumption doesn't do justice to the facts. Professor Flew admits that in such a case the presuppositions of historical explanation and reconstruction, which are otherwise successfully applied, may be challenged and perhaps must be broadened: "corrected and supplemented." Obviously the historian will be reluctant to do so if there are alternative means of explanation at hand. Whether the Christian message of the Resurrection of Jesus provides one of those rare occasions that expose an unjustified narrowness in the principles of historical method must be checked by looking at the evidence.

This was done, then, by both participants in the debate. And it is at this point that weak elements in Professor Flew's procedure become apparent. In the first place, there is a lack of sophistication in his way of dealing with the biblical reports. Quite obviously, Professor Habermas is far better informed about the details of historical scholarship concerning the early Christian traditions relating to the Easter events. Professor Flew knows that the Pauline account on the appearances of the risen Christ in 1 Corinthians 15 is the oldest available text. He is generous concerning the date of 1 Corinthians when he allows for a date as early as ten years after the Crucifixion of Jesus, and the date of Paul's first missionary activity is pretty clear from the reference to Gallio in Acts 18:12 combined with the famous Gallio inscription, the basis of the whole modern chronology of Paul's career. That means that the first letter to the Corinthians cannot be earlier than the middle A.D. 50s. But on the other hand, there are reasons to conclude that the information on the appearances of the risen Jesus must be much older.

First, in 1 Corinthians 15:1 and 3, Paul explicitly emphasizes the traditional character of the following information, and the language of the subsequent formula or formulae is formalized into a creed. The reactions of Professor Flew to the repeated emphasis put on this fact by Professor Habermas seem to indicate that he is aware neither of the extensive discussion on this particular text nor of the consequences following from the formalized nature of these phrases in connection with, second, the information given by Paul himself (Gal. 1:18 sq.) on his early contact with the Jerusalem community, especially with Peter and James. Even if the creedal formula (or formalized pieces) of 1 Corinthians 15:3b–5 (7) was delivered, as some scholars say, to Paul at Antioch, the community that first sent him out as a missionary, there is still every reason to assume that Paul on occasion of his personal contact with Peter and James at Jerusalem three years after his conversion (Gal. 1:18) got firsthand confirmation of the content of that tradition. Professor Flew is correct that over the course of ten years the content of a story can be substantially transformed, especially when extraordinary events are reported and when the process of tradition is anonymous. But he did not pay due attention to the concrete circumstances of this case, as Professor Habermas correctly insists. Therefore, Flew's emphasis on the comparatively late character of the documents concerning Jesus' Resurrection, even of 1 Corinthians, is not very persuasive. It would be quite different if Paul had simply reported by hearsay, but this is not so.

The weakness of Professor Flew's argument in terms of historical detail damages his position because he admits that no a priori decision of the issue is acceptable and that the case must be settled on the basis of the evidence. Professor Flew argues that there is simply not enough evidence and not the kind of evidence required to tell what really happened, but one expects that he should at least take notice of the evidence at hand and that he should do so in detail as well as by informing himself on the scholarly discussion of it. Otherwise, the skeptical claim that the evidence is insufficient smacks of the kind of a priori rejection that Professor Flew disclaims.

Another problem with that skeptical attitude is that in some cases it becomes logically impossible to suspend judgment. It is, of course, possible to forgo truth claims of individuals or institutions, if one is not concerned. But in the case of historical reconstruction, one cannot leave all questions regarding the relevant facts in suspense and still offer a reconstruction of that particular process. Many particulars may be left in suspense, but a decision on the events deemed relevant and essential to the process in question must be made. Thus it is impossible to account for the early history of Christianity without making up one's mind on the Easter tradition. In cases such as this even the avoidance of a decision amounts to a decision: if one treats the reports on Jesus' Resurrection as merely beliefs of the early Christians, then the question must be answered as to how these people came to hold those beliefs. If an answer to that question is refused, then what in fact is said is that those beliefs are treated as products of human imagination and that understanding the way the beliefs were formed is not essential for understanding the emergence of Christianity.

In most details of the historical argument I agree with Professor Habermas, especially in his discussion of Paul's connection with Jerusalem concerning his list of appearances of the risen Jesus, although I am less certain than he about the homogeneity of 1 Corinthians 15:3b–5 (7). Rather than being a single creed, this passage may contain different fragments put together by Paul himself on the occasion of this letter. But even in this case the fragments still show formalized language. Further, I agree with Professor Habermas's list of twelve facts relating to the Easter events that are admitted by most scholars, with the exception (as he himself says) of the empty-tomb tradition, which I do, however, consider as historical in its core. In what sense the historicity of the Resurrection can be demonstrated on the basis of these facts will be discussed later on. Even Professor Flew admits that the textual authority concerning these events, as compared to many other pieces of information about ancient history, is "unusually great." I certainly concur with Professor Habermas in his confidence that a strong argument in favor of the historicity of the Resurrection of Jesus can be given. Whether it amounts to a "demonstration" depends on what one understands by that term. I also agree that such an argument cannot be effectively rebuked by referring to the discrepancies in the biblical reports, especially in the stories of the Gospels. Because the argument can be based on those twelve facts that most historians accept, it is largely independent of those discrepancies. I doubt, however, if the four core historical facts referred to by Professor Habermas could carry the weight of such an argument. What is decisive in historical argument is not some isolated piece of evidence, but rather the convergence of all the available evidence and of the interpretations that can be based on such evidence. Therefore, the argument is conclusive only in view of all the available evidence and upon due consideration of the relevant circumstances.

The argument for a literal Resurrection depends on the convergence of the reports on appearances with the empty-tomb tradition. If we had only the reports on appearances of the risen Lord, these phenomena— however explained—would not need to be related to the dead body of Jesus and to a transformation of that body, although the Jewish conception of a resurrection definitely is concerned with the body. The body reference in the Jewish conception of resurrection justifies the conclusion that Paul, in speaking of Christ as having been dead and buried and risen, assumed by implication that he could no longer occupy his tomb. For the same reason it is difficult to imagine the early apostolic proclamation of Jesus as risen to have taken place at Jerusalem without his tomb being empty. In all these points I share the position taken by Professor Habermas in his dispute with Professor Flew. Still, however, the assumption of a literal Resurrection (even in terms of a transformation to some new and immortal form of life) is dependent —as far as historical judgment is concerned—on the evaluation of the tomb tradition and on the fact that traces of early Christian apologetics against Jewish critics of the message of Jesus' Resurrection (Matt. 28:13sqq., John 20:15) suggest that even the critics took the fact of the empty tomb for granted and differed only in the explanation of it. Thus the question of the empty tomb shows that the final judgment must be based on the convergence of the evidence. Similarly, the empty tomb taken by itself cannot provide a conclusive argument for the Resurrection of Jesus. This was already expressed by Luke's Gospel when the discovery of the tomb to be empty caused mere bewilderment among the disciples (cf. Lk. 24:22sq.); the appearances of the risen Jesus first revealed to the disciples that he was alive. Therefore the case for the

Resurrection rests primarily with the appearances, but the judgment concerning the kind of reality that occurred with the appearances cannot be independent of the question of what happened to the tomb. Therefore this tradition has often been the object of excessive skepticism in modern scholarship. If one accepts the empty-tomb tradition, one is pushed to a literal conception of Resurrection, so in liberal theology that particular tradition was not very popular. But Hans von Campenhausen, a liberal historian himself, has pointed out the difficulties of theories that take Mark 16:1–8 as a late Hellenistic legend: if it were such, the text should look different in a number of details, especially regarding the role ascribed to women, who at that time were not considered reliable witnesses, and also in view of the fact that the old report ending with Mark 16:8 did not include an appearance story. Because, however, the text resists the kind of critical description offered by Bultmann and others, the more general observation that the proclamation of Jesus' Resurrection hardly could have developed and prospered at Jerusalem, the place of his Crucifixion and burial, if his tomb had not been empty, gains its full weight together with the absence of any insinuation in Jewish sources that his body remained in its tomb or that the tomb was not known.

There is only one major point where I cannot share the historical argument presented by Professor Habermas. This concerns the form of the appearances of the risen Lord. Here I sympathize with the view of Professor Flew, derived perhaps from M. C. Perry, that Paul's experience of the risen Jesus cannot have been altogether different from the appearances that occurred to Peter, James, and the other apostles. Professor Habermas does not accept this, and the Gospels, especially Luke, present the reality of the Risen One in a much more earthly fashion than the report in Acts on Paul's conversion by the light and the voice coming to him from heaven (Acts 9:3sqq., 22:6sqq., and 26:12sqq.). The Easter narratives in the Gospels, however, represent a much later stage of the tradition than Paul's own remark (Gal. 1:15), which fits with the story in Acts. It has often been noticed that in the process of the Easter tradition the latest version, in the apocryphal Gospel of Peter, displays the most massive realism in its description. By contrast, Mark 16:1–8 shows the highest degree of restraint. It seems that the realism of the appearances and of the bodily reality of the Risen One was increasingly emphasized in the course of the development of that tradition. The apologetic pressures to that effect are understandable. Therefore, although recent scholarship has suggested that the Resurrection narratives of the Gospels should not be judged as historically worthless, it is not possible to deny legendary elements in those narratives, especially in their final form, representing comparatively late stages of their tradition. Therefore, I could not consider the Gospels in every respect as historically reliable sources, as Professor Habermas says they are. Unlike Professor Habermas, I share the doubts of most scholars concerning the Gospel reports after Mark 8:31, 9:31, and 10:34 that Jesus predicted his own Resurrection.

That Resurrection meant a most powerful confirmation of Jesus' claim to authority, which may have been more implicit in the way he preached the kingdom than the Gospels present it to us, is not dependent on such an assumption. The general nature of the Gospel reports, then, does not allow us to take them directly as historical sources, although they certainly include valid points of historical information. This especially applies to the Easter narratives, where the diversity and discrepancy is greater than in most areas of the Gospel tradition. Therefore the presentation of the appearances of the risen Lord, for example, in the Gospel of Luke, does not stand on the same footing as the reports on Paul's experience in Acts. When Luke in his Gospel presents the appearances to the disciples as being in a different form than the one experienced by Paul according to Acts, it may be because he tends to elevate the authority of the twelve (or eleven) who knew Jesus from his pre-Easter ministry above that of the missionaries of the early church, including Paul (although otherwise Luke honors the unique importance of Paul's work in the history of early Christian missions). Paul himself, however, emphasized that the apostolic authority of his ministry was equal to that of the leading apostles of Jerusalem, and he obtained some degree of recognition of his claims at the so-called Jerusalem synod (Acts 15). But because his claim to apostolic authority was bound up with his experience of an appearance of the risen Lord, the recognition of his position by the others was closely related to the question of whether his experience was similar to theirs and sufficiently different from later visionary experiences. Therefore the fact of Paul's recognition at Jerusalem strongly suggests that what can be found out about Paul's experience may also apply, in a general way, to the original form of the appearances of others, such as Peter and James. Even at a late stage of the tradition of the Easter narratives as represented by the Gospels, it is still preserved, as Professor Habermas mentions, that the body of the Risen One is considered a transformed reality, not unlike what Paul says in 1 Corinthians 15:42sqq. on the "spiritual body" of the new life of the Resurrection in contrast with the present condition of bodily existence.

When Professor Flew refers to those "puzzling paragraphs about corruption taking on incorruption" he has every right to wonder what kind of reality Paul had in mind. But he certainly misses Paul's point when he submits the suggestion that a "spiritual body" may simply amount to a contradiction in terms similar to an "unmarried husband." He asks what difference there is between a spiritual body and a nonexistent one. In terms of Paul's own conception this question can be answered as soon as one takes into account that in Jewish tradition the concept of spirit was different from that of certain Greek philosophers. In the Hebrew Bible, God's Spirit was regarded as the source of life (for example, Gen. 2:7 and Ps. 104:30). The present life, because it is mortal, is not fully united with that divine origin of life. In other words, our share in the Spirit is limited, and therefore we die. This description provides the background for the meaning of Paul's conception of a spiritual life (or body), which means a form of life that is no longer separated from the divine origin of life and hence is immortal, as Paul says (1 Cor. 15:42, 52sqq.). This explanation may not convey all the information we would like to have on that new form of the life to come, but it is enough to distinguish Paul's conception of a "spiritual body" from a contradiction in terms. The emphasis is that not some part of our present existence will be transformed into everlasting life, and this also provides a clue as to how Paul understood the reality of the risen Lord, whom he had encountered on the road to Damascus.

Finally, I return to the question of historicity. Earlier I granted Professor Flew's point that the credibility of exceptional events requires stronger evidence than do reports on the kinds of events that happen every day. Does the investigation of the early Christian Easter tradition provide evidence of such a kind? The answer is both yes and no. Yes, because of the positive results that an unprejudiced examination of the sources produces. The weakness of Professor Flew's position in the dispute with Professor Habermas was his a priori assumption of the inconclusive character of the evidence and his reluctance to enter into a serious discussion of the historical detail. On this level there is a good deal to say in favor of the historical soundness of the apostolic claim that Jesus was indeed raised from the dead and proved himself alive to his disciples and to Paul and James. But after all that is said, there is still the issue that Professor Flew pointed to on several occasions: in the world of our ordinary experience, dead persons do not leave their graves, not even in exceptional cases, and because of this it is hard to believe that it happened to Jesus. At some points in the discourse Professor Flew came close to saying that if that were otherwise there would be no problem with the condition of the historical sources we have. Even the case of the Jewish contemporaries of Jesus—including his disciples and apostles—was different from the situation of the modern historian in that they shared the traditionally Jewish belief in God's powerful dominion over the course of events, free to interfere at whatever point he pleased. Thus the point of view that Cardinal Newman sought to reestablish in terms of natural theology was taken for granted in the Jewish tradition. In addition, the most important section of Judaism at the time of early Christian history, the Pharisaic movement, shared with the Christians the expectation of a final Resurrection of the dead at the end of the present world, when God's kingdom would come to power. The secular historian can no longer take this framework for granted. But neither did naturalistic historians succeed in explaining the historical evidence of the Easter tradition in even a half-way satisfactory form. It has been said rightly that the legends created by excessive criticism have been less credible than the biblical reports themselves. Therefore the historical solidity of the Christian witness poses a considerable challenge to the conception of reality that is taken for granted by modern secular history. There are good and even superior reasons for claiming that the Resurrection of

Jesus was a historical event, and consequently the risen Lord himself is a living reality. And yet there is the innumerably repeated experience that in this world the dead do not rise again. As long as this is the case, the Christian affirmation of Jesus' Resurrection will remain a debated issue, in spite of all sound historical argument as to its historicity. Although Christians should never lose their nerve in this matter but insist on the historicity of Jesus' Resurrection as long as the evidence warrants such a claim, they also should not be surprised that only in the kingdom to come, when the dead rise again, will the opposition to their claim vanish.

NOTES

1. Wolfhart Pannenberg, *Jesus—God and Man* trans. Lewis T. Wilkins and Duane A. Priebe (Philadelphia: Westminster Press, 1968).
2. H. v. Campenhausen, *Der Ablauf der Osterereignisse und das leere Grab* (1952).
3. The last words in David Hume's section "Of Miracles" in his *Enquiry concerning human understanding* (London, 1748).

Charles Hartshorne

Dr. Johnson, as given to us by Boswell, based his Christian faith on the Resurrection. So did my father, a man so far ahead of his time that in the 1880s he accepted evolution while preparing himself to be an Episcopal clergyman. I cannot, however, agree with these two in this matter. Indeed, my belief in God, and in the service of God as the meaning of life, is not based on any historical occurrences, however remarkable. (I largely agree with Hume, as did Charles Peirce, that we must balance the probability of recorded miraculous happenings against the probability that those who tell us about the happenings were above making mistakes in their acceptance of indirect evidence.) All the religions tell of miracles. Buddha was "born speaking"; when the Japanese Buddhist saint Shotaku Taishi died, "rain fell from cloudless skies." I do not feel that I can choose among such accounts and base my life on the results. I admit that, as my father thought, it is remarkable that a crucified man should have been the source of so vast a company of believers. I cannot explain this convincingly. But then I cannot explain how Buddhism or other religions grew as they did.

There is another consideration. I do not seek, or feel a need for, belief in survival of death—in a career beyond the grave for myself or other human animals. For me, God is the genuinely immortal being, and my everlastingness is neither more nor less than my entire earthly career as contribution to the divine life. God cherishes all the creatures for what they are, and in this way each makes an imperishable contribution to the embracing consciousness, or (Karl Jaspers) "the Encompassing One." I have no religious use, only an esthetic use, for Dante's or Augustine's deprecation of life on this planet in comparison to life on a new supernatural plane and in a new and deathless body (or as a mere disembodied soul).

A human personality is for me like a theme in a work of art; themes normally admit of only a limited number of nontrivial variations.

Hence the finitude of our lives in space-time is as it should be. Only one theme is significantly variable beyond finite limits, the divine personality or superpersonality. How this can be so in one superbeing is mysterious enough, but it makes more sense to me than a similar claim for each human animal's, or any human animal's, personality.

A technical point is that I accept, with minor qualifications, Karl Popper's view that empirical evidence (and what knowledge we have of the life of Jesus is empirical) is not sufficient for all our cognitive needs. Not every important belief is falsifiable by conceivable observation. Belief in God is such a belief. I reject the dogma that only conceivably falsifiable statements can assert existence. I hold that no conceivable observation could falsify "something exists." Yet the statement is true. "There might have been nothing" sounds like an affirmation, but is really nonsense. No observation could show that "nothing is"; the word *nothing* is idling when so used. Henri Bergson has made this clear. I hold that the idea of God, properly explicated, gives the content of the Something that there *must* be, and not simply God solus, but God with some world or other.

The foregoing hinted-at ontological argument is one of six reasons I have for being a theist. None of them is an appeal to particular observations; all are appeals to concepts without which we cannot adequately deal with life's problems, intelligibly explicate our aim in life, or explain how not just our world but any world can exist and have meaning and value.

I wonder how many philosophers are aware of the privilege philosophers now have with respect to nonempirical, metaphysical problems. We have, as no philosophers did have until recently, the advantage that every combination of certain basic ideas has by now been tried. Consider the ideas, God, and individual human posthumous careers. The Jains and a few Westerners (J. M. E. McTaggart was an example) accept the second but reject the first. For me, they confirm my contention that wanting to be immortal in the specified sense is a form of wanting to be God. It makes one a rival of deity. A brilliant contemporary (who was briefly a student of mine) believes in God but only on condition that he can trust God to give him survival, a posthumous career. I call this making bargains with deity. On the other hand, he argues, with some cogency, that theism gives one a plus in living. He is a man well instructed in the hard sciences, mathematics, and physics.

McTaggart and my ornithologist friend are inclined to accept determinism, McTaggart emphatically so. Now if I know anything philosophical, I know that determinism is not simply false, but a piece of bad metaphysics. It belongs with other concepts of the Newtonian era, and both physics and metaphysics have moved beyond that system of ideas. I hold that the combination that until the last twelve decades or so was scarcely tried by anyone is now the best bet: God, no immortality other than Whiteheadian objective immortality in the Consequent nature of God, and creative freedom transcending, however slightly, causal necessities not simply in human beings but in all dynamic singulars in nature—particles, atoms, plant and animal cells, many-celled animals. I claim to have proved that freedom entails an aspect of chance, as Epicurus by implication said it did long ago. God, determinism, endless careers for human beings, these have been combined over and over in the past; it is time to try the combination God, finite careers for human beings, and freedom (with chance as well as partial necessity).

It debases theistic belief to regard God as a supernatural means for our escape from the only mode of nondivine individual existence that we know (with doubly finite durations, careers that begin as well as end). Not only the idea of God is thus distorted, that of mind and consciousness in general is also. Either we posit disembodied spirits, as though we knew at all what these would be like, or we posit bodies with no real analogy to anything we know. And God becomes the supreme disembodied spirit.

There is a better way. According to it, our survival of death is not in a new career that we will enjoy but in God's everlasting enjoyment of our earthly careers. Not our enjoyment, in ever new ways, of God and the creation, is our immortality, but God's ever-new enjoyment of us in contrast with new creatures as these come into being. This has analogy to the way we enjoy shorter-lived creatures, including our own bodily cells.

What do we have from this "objective immortality"? Alfred North Whitehead has given the answer; apart from objective immortality, our moments of experience are but passing whiffs of insignificance. Where are the joys of yesteryear? What does it matter how happy or unhappy we were? With objective immortality our fleeting days acquire lasting significance. If people can live or die for country, or other human group, why can they not live and die for that which embraces all groups and their intrinsic values—the divine life? That we should love God with all our being can then be taken literally. Only if we love God, who loves us incomparably better than we can love ourselves or our mortal friends, can we really love anything or anyone fully knowing what we are doing, because if any good is there for us to love, it is permanently cherished and given lasting status only as loved by the divine consciousness.

For indulging in dreams of heaven and nightmares of hell, Christians and followers of Muhammad have paid a high price. I admire the ancient and many modern Jews who have worshiped God (see the Book of Job) without asking for posthumous rewards, or acting from fear of posthumous punishments.

Part of the cost of despising the human body is that it forces us to render dubious in the extreme the analogy theism assumes between the human mind and God. What our awareness would be like without its everpresent relations to its bodily cells, we have only blind guesses. Moreover, it is not a question of relating mind on our human level with mere dead, mindless matter, for that negative notion is a construct, not a datum or object of scientific knowledge. Physicists have not undertaken to prove that cells or even atoms are totally mindless. Gottfried Wilhelm Leibniz, Charles S. Peirce, Alfred North Whitehead, and many of lesser fame have been physicists who believed that matter is a primitive form of mind. The greatest biologist I have known believes this. Several important psychologists have believed it. There is nothing in science that I know of that forbids us from taking our relations to the microconstituents of our bodies to be other than relations of mind or spirit on our level with a multitude of much less intellectual, or, in the pregnant sense, conscious, but still sentient little beings, cells (or constituents thereof). In that way we can return to Plato's World Soul idea and give new meaning to it, thanks to modern science. Whitehead did not, but I do, agree with Plato that if we posit a divine analogue to our minds, then we should posit such an analogue to our bodies. And, unlike Plato, we know what only Epicurus guessed in ancient times, that Plato's criterion of soul or mind in the most general sense —self-motion or self-change—applies to all the singular constituents of physical things, where sticks and stones are not singulars but collectives. Even trees, Whitehead says, are collectives ("a tree is a democracy"). What Whitehead failed to see but helped me to see is that Plato's World Soul (as F. M. Cornford interprets it) can, in the light of quantum physics, do what it could not do so long as self-change was supposed to be confined to plants and animals. There is no inert matter and no unorganized, "inorganic" matter either; everywhere there is self-change (Whitehead's "creativity" or Bergson's or Peirce's "spontaneity"). So who can claim to know that there is any mindless matter? And so we can, improving upon Plato, think of God's love for us as an eminent analogue of our largely unconscious love for our cells. Whitehead virtually does this when not evaluating Platonism.

I once discussed objective immortality with Reinhold Niebuhr, who said that he was not prepared to say that a Christian could not take Whitehead's view on this question, but added that he preferred to leave the religious meaning of death an unrationalized mystery. Read Paul Tillich, and I think you will find that he too does not definitely reject the Whiteheadian view. At last we begin, in the philosophy of religion, to move out of the medieval and Newtonian prison—for Newton did not attribute self-change to atoms, which he thought were moved only by God. Epicurus thought otherwise. His own awareness consisted, he held, of atoms, and because he was sure he had genuine freedom, he thought the atoms had a little of it. He failed to see that his materialism was open to refutation by the same type of argument that upsets determinism.

If these remarks are too brief to be convincing, the works of Peirce, Whitehead, myself, and others can give them a more supportive context than is possible here.

As to the New Testament Resurrection story, the swoon theory, which was discussed in the question and answer period, says that Jesus may have been only apparently dead at the end of the terrible hours on the Cross and may have revived later in the tomb and lived for a few weeks longer. I neither believe nor disbelieve this hypothesis. I simply wonder if we can ever know. John Hick expects to know when he awakes in heaven. He thinks this odd situation makes the matter an empirical question. But I use words as Popper has suggested. *Empirical* means "falsifiable by observation." Only conceptual arguments can give reasons for denying Hick's hypothesis. But I for one fail to see how either observation or conceptual arguments can really show what Hick wants in this matter. Even if one does find "oneself" experiencing in heaven, this only shows that natural death is not the absolute end of a career. Supposing natural life to be followed by supernatural life, supernatural life could end in some equally supernatural death. Observation can only show finite, not infinite, extension of a career. I think we should leave immortality, other than objective, to God. In this I am agreeing with Peirce, Whitehead, and Bergson.

I find that my essay is rather marginal to the historical issues discussed in the debate. What I have said will, I think, make clear why it is apart from my main concern. I can neither explain away the evidences to which Habermas appeals, nor can I simply agree with Flew's or Hume's positions. I believe in a basic and divinely inspired cosmic order, but I also believe, with Peirce, Whitehead, and many other philosophers and physicists, that (Whitehead) "disorder is as real as order." There is disorder because there is universal creativity; there is order because supreme creativity inspires all actualities with feeling for its vision of the cosmic patterns so far as relevant to them. All this is too complicated to explain further here.

A final remark: I strongly incline to believe in rational inhabitants of some other planets. My view is not humanistic and earth-centered, but cosmic and God-centered; theomorphic, not anthropomorphic. God and some cosmos or other is the presupposition of all thought, not our species and its world. Our human symbolic power, ability to abstract and generalize, enables us to transcend (fallibly and in outline only) some aspects of our animal limitations.

My metaphysical bias is against resurrections.

James I. Packer

Christianity is like no other faith on earth, and those who try to assimilate it to the rest of the religions, speaking of them as if they reflect or foreshadow it or of it as reflecting or foreshadowing them, are flying in the face of the facts. Whether you compare Christianity with Judaism or Islam, its hostile half-brothers, or with Hinduism and its atheistic child Buddhism, or with Taoism or state Shintoism or any type of polytheism, or with any other religion that humanity has developed, the basic contrast is invariably the same. Non-Christian faiths have an inner structure different from Christianity, for they all ring changes on the theme of self-salvation. They offer ultimate happiness, however they conceive it, as a prize to be gained from God, or the gods, or the cosmic order, through knowledgeable and worthy action on our part. This is the universal formula of natural religion. But Christianity, which sees ultimate happiness as rescue from sin and an unending love relationship with one's Creator, offers this salvation package as a gift, to be received here and now by admitting our helplessness and entering into a faith relationship with Jesus Christ, the divine-human Savior and Lord.

When Christians are asked to make good their claim that this scheme is truth, they point to Jesus' Resurrection. The Easter event, so they affirm, demonstrated Jesus' deity; validated his teaching; attested the completion of his work of atonement for sin; confirms his present cosmic dominion and his coming reappearance as Judge; assures us that his personal pardon, presence, and power in people's lives today is fact; and guarantees each believer's own reembodiment by Resurrection in the world to come. Such is the significance of Jesus' bodily Resurrection in the eyes of Christians. From it they learn that Jesus is not just a historical memory, one who is dead yet speaks as model and mentor, like Abel, but that he is a living Savior, a loving Master, and an everlasting friend to all who trust him. They think of him so; they relate to him so; they sing and pray to him accordingly; they say with Paul that Christ is their life and their hope. So naturally they perceive any questioning of the historical reality of Jesus' Resurrection as an attempt to knock the bottom out of their faith.

Nor are they wrong. This is what for the past two centuries a large company of professional history writers in the West, sometimes within though more often outside the church, has been doing. Embracing a methodology that insists on explaining everything in naturalistic terms (that is, in terms of regularities within the system observed in parallel cases), and that dismisses other sorts of explanation (the Creator's creative action, for instance) as superstitious and naive, history writing of this kind accounts for the New Testament witness to the empty tomb, the appearances of the risen Lord, and the subsequent advance of Christianity in a way that implies delusion on the part of those who believe.

Christians have reacted in different ways. Some, such as Karl Barth, disengage from the debate about Christian origins, dismissing this rationalistic skepticism as indicating a spiritual blindness that may be left to God to deal with, and meantime carrying on regardless of it. The weakness there is that refusal to answer points put in the name of historical reason looks like an admission that one has no answer to them, and thus that faith is an irrational commitment that closes the mind to evidence. That does not honor God! Others, such as Bishop David Jenkins of Durham, England, whom Professor Flew mentions in his opening remarks, seek ways of affirming the risenness of Jesus that do not involve an empty tomb or veridical appearances of a Resurrection body. These then get assaulted both by believers, for now believing too little, and by unbelievers, for still believing too much, and it has to be said that their timid, arbitrary compromises, masquerading as they do as bold enlightened syntheses, deserve every bit of the kicking that they receive from both sides. Halfway houses, erected by means of unprincipled concessions, do not honor God either!

Other Christians, however, fight back, having woken up not only to the need to honor God by vindicating the historical facts on which faith rests, but also to the strength of the historical case that is theirs to argue against skepticism about the Resurrection. "You have appealed to history; to history you shall go." A steady flow of books in this century has shown over and over again that you cannot reasonably deny Jesus' Resurrection on a posteriori grounds—that is, by maintaining that another explanation of the evidence fits better. Denial of the Resurrection can be made to seem reasonable only on a priori grounds —that is, by assuming, as rationalist-positivist historians do assume, that only parallel cases, real or imagined, within the system constitute explanation, and by ruling out in advance creative acts of God in his world.

It is no wonder then, that Christians, having appreciated the cogency of their own case, should seek opportunities to show it, nor that they should welcome public debate as one such opportunity. Debate, or disputation, to give it its older name, is a form of structured discussion inherited from the medieval universities that aims to educate in three ways. First, it gets all relevant arguments out on the table, to be tested for strength by seeing what can be said for and against them. Second, it disciplines the disputants themselves, honing their powers of analysis, argument, and riposte. Third, it instructs spectators in the complexities and simplicities of the issues under dispute. It is not ordinarily expected that disputants will change their position while the debate is on; the ethics of debate are, rather, that one makes the best case one can at the outset and defends it throughout against criticism as well as one can, so that observers may be able to gauge how much truth there is on each side. For a good debate, the disputants need to be competent and well briefed on the matter at hand, and the topic needs to be one that admits of clear definition. The debate structure is obviously well suited to exploring the issue between those who think it unreasonable to believe that Jesus rose from the dead and those who think it unreasonable not to do so, and one expects a high quality of argument from any parties involved in this discussion.

There is, however, a built-in limitation: you can debate only one question at a time. If, as in the present exchange, the question is the historicity of Jesus' Resurrection—that is, the adequacy of the grounds for believing that Jesus rose bodily from the dead—then the question cannot at the same time be the theological significance of the Resurrection, or its importance for humanity. Flew is right to say at the outset that belief in Jesus' Resurrection is the necessary precondition of belief in his divinity, but it needs to be remembered that belief in Jesus' Resurrection does not logically require this further belief, nor do all who believe in the Resurrection actually affirm Jesus' divinity in the Christian sense of that word. Examples of this are New Age teachers, for whom Jesus could rise because he was a supreme mystical adept, and the Jewish theologian Pinchas Lapide, who wrote *The Resurrection of Jesus: A Jewish Perspective.* [1] The exclusion from this present discussion of Christian concerns about the meaning of the Resurrection was inevitable, just because the factuality of the Resurrection was the selected issue, and no one should bewail the omission, as if within the debate's fixed terms of reference something else had been possible. It was not. As Gertrude Stein might have said, Debate is debate is debate. And in debate, as in golf, you must keep your eye on the ball.

The other limits, though, that seem to have been imposed by mutual agreement—that the existence of God and the reasons distinct from and antecedent to the Resurrection for believing in Jesus' divinity would not be discussed—were not strictly necessary and are regrettable. For what is involved here is not the question itself, but the range of arguments that each side might use in exploring it. Professor Flew's easy dismissal of Newman's response to Hume would not have been possible apart from these limitations, nor would he have been free simply to shrug off the correspondence between the empty tomb and the recorded post-Resurrection utterances of Jesus and things he is reported as having said and done before his arrest and death. Professor Habermas mentions some of this, and it does in fact add up to a strong argument both for Jesus' personal deity (that originally unthinkable and unspeakably shocking conviction to which his Jewish followers were finally driven) and for his Resurrection as a fact, unexpected, at first unbelievable, but yet undeniable. One wishes that these considerations could have been brought into the debate directly; the case for Jesus' Resurrection cannot be fully mounted until they are.

A further limitation that appears is that the form of the debate itself was awkwardly loose. No doubt it was a personal courtesy to Professor Flew to ask him to speak first, but it queered the pitch. The first speaker in a debate normally asserts something that the second speaker then denies. To have the first speaker spend all his strength negating in advance what he expects the next speaker to say is never the best way to open up a subject, and in this instance the announced subject, the historicity of Jesus' Resurrection, does not get fully opened up at any stage. Professor Flew, whose position throughout the debate appears as one not of dogmatic denial but of dogmatic agnosticism regarding the Resurrection, does in fact assert something: namely, that the New Testament evidence is necessarily and intrinsically inadequate to warrant our saying whether Jesus rose from the dead the third day. To this Professor Habermas replies that this evidence is in fact overwhelming, justifying certainty as to the fact and making doubts about it unreasonable. The quality of the evidence continues to be Flew's main concern; he argues constantly that statements dating from as little as ten years after the event, when made by believers in it, must be judged late and unreliable, and that Paul's vision of the risen Christ on the road to Damascus can be accounted for without positing the mind-independent reality of Jesus in his Resurrection body being "there" for Paul to see. The quantity of the evidence continues to be Habermas's concern; he argues constantly that the cumulative weight of it, as the separate pieces interlock, is conclusive, whatever queries might be raised about this or that item of it. Flew focuses on the knowability of the Resurrection, even supposing it to be fact (which he sees no reason to grant), rather than directly debating its factuality as such.

Uncertainty as to whether the state of the question under debate is whether Jesus actually rose, or whether, supposing that he did, the New Testament justifies confidence that he did, persists to the end, and the discussion oscillates accordingly. One might have expected Flew to attack Habermas for using evidence uncritically, but he does not do so; nor does Habermas hammer Flew for not facing evidence, and thus in effect doing what he said he would not do, that is, rejecting the Resurrection on a priori grounds ("such things don't happen, whatever you say, and that's that"). Polite people pull punches! The sustained friendliness of the exchange is admirable in itself, but a less friendly discussion would help more.

Flew's casualness, in particular, is to be regretted. A distinguished positivist logician and historian of philosophy by trade, he limits himself to making general negative points about (1) the antecedent impossibility of positing a miracle when a purposeful divine miracle worker is not posited; (2) the antecedent impropriety of believing the witness of interested parties ten or more years after the event (Why? I can remember vividly unusual things that happened ten, twenty, thirty, and forty years ago, and so, no doubt, can Flew); (3) the formal nonidentity and nonequivalence of hearsay evidence received from eyewitnesses and the testimony of those witnesses themselves (a point weighty in law, but trivial here, as in most of life); and (4) the possibility of Paul's experience on the road to Damascus, plus other experiences of meeting the risen Lord, being hallucinations of a kind not well understood. He does not appear to have briefed himself on any of the technical discussion by modern scholars of the first-century background and the New Testament documents, preferring to deal with everything in the informal conversational style of an Oxford senior common room discussion over the port. The technical excellence of Habermas's carefully prepared material makes the inappropriateness of this procedure obvious.

Certainly Flew's position as he sets it up is impregnable. If God's existence may not be discussed or presupposed, then the possibility of Jesus' Resurrection has to be approached as an argument for, rather than from or within, a theistic view of the universe; but the evidence for the empty tomb and Resurrection appearances, taken in isolation, can hardly be treated as conclusive evidence for theism, whatever force it may have for those who are theists already. Were this evidence set in the context of Israel's history and faith and Jesus' life and teaching, the case would be altered, but the agreed limitations on the debate have ruled that out. Again, if only uncommitted or hostile witnesses count and testimony from interested parties does not count, then there is no real evidence for Jesus' Resurrection. And once more, if the category of hallucination may be extended at will beyond anything that psychologists have yet been able to observe and describe (a hazardous play, surely, for a positivist, whose method is to define possibility in terms of actuality as scientists know it—but let that pass), then there is no difficulty in accounting for the Resurrection appearances. There is no question that these stage settings make Flew's position impregnable ("can't catch me"); the only question is whether a stance thus defined and circumscribed can be thought of as reasonable. Let the reader judge.

The case for the historical reality of Jesus' bodily Resurrection could be made even stronger than Professor Habermas makes it—which, in all conscience, must surely be strong enough already for most people! —by dwelling with more emphasis on the sheer impossibility of accounting for the triumphant emergence of Christianity in Jerusalem, a faith based on acknowledging Jesus as crucified Messiah and risen Lord, without the supposition that his tomb was found mysteriously empty. If the authorities could have produced Jesus' corpse, they would have exploded the Resurrection faith for good; the fact that it was not exploded indicates that they did not produce the corpse, and their failure to produce it, even without Matthew's statement that they started a rumor that the disciples had stolen it, shows that they could not produce it. The idea that those who constantly risked their freedom and their lives proclaiming the Resurrection faith had in fact stolen the body, and therefore knew all along that their preaching was not true, is unbelievable. One of the tasks of history writing is to identify the causes of events, and one of the marks of good historians is that they show themselves aware of what constitutes a cause, or set of causes, commensurate with what actually happened. What happened here is that Christianity actually started with the Resurrection. This is the great fact (too great, apparently, for Flew even to notice) by which the adequacy of any view about Jesus' rising must finally be judged. Claims to have seen Jesus after his death could not have started such a faith had Jesus' corpse been available for inspection, for claims by the recently bereaved to have had contact with the departed one do not impress while the latter's body molders in the grave. To posit the emptiness of the tomb is thus a rational necessity, for the rise of Christianity is inexplicable otherwise.

Adducing the Shroud of Turin does not, however, strengthen the case for Jesus' Resurrection. If on other grounds one already believes that Jesus rose, it then makes sense to ask whether the marks on the shroud might have been made by the rising process, and in the light of one's guesses about that (for guesses are all that is possible) to estimate the likelihood of this being Jesus' burial cloth. Until Jesus'

Resurrection is established on other grounds, however, the shroud is not evidence for anything, but is just a tantalizing medieval oddity: no more.

It is a truism that argument alone does not make Christians. "Convince a man against his will, he's of the same opinion still," says the wise old couplet, and what Flew calls the "unsanctified eye" notoriously fails to see what is there before it. Christians know that without prevenient grace no one recognizes the full force of God-given evidence about Jesus so as to come to the knowledge of God's saving truth. This is supremely the case with Jesus' Resurrection. But argument can show the unreasonableness of unbelief, and demonstrate that there is more of prejudice and credulity involved in rejecting Christian beliefs than in accepting them, and that, if not everything, is at least something. This too is supremely the case with Jesus' Resurrection. The present debate, taken as a whole, seems to me to contribute something of substance that vividly illustrates this truth, and I am glad that it is going to be made public for all to see. For, as Flew rightly says, more rightly perhaps than he himself perceives, the matter is one "of supreme theoretical and practical importance."

NOTES

1. Pinchas Lapide, *The Resurrection of Jesus: A Jewish Perspective* (Minneapolis: Augsburg, 1983).

IV. A FINAL RESPONSE

Some Final Thoughts on the Resurrection: Gary R. Habermas

I was asked to write a reply to the three respondents whose comments on the debate are included in this book. I would first like to express my thanks to Professors Wolfhart Pannenberg, Charles Hartshorne, and James Packer for setting aside their work to provide their analysis for this debate. It is true that, in general, formulating a reply helps to clarify one's position; I trust this will be the case here.

PROFESSOR WOLFHART PANNENBERG

Professor Pannenberg's response contained many welcome compliments concerning most of the major points in my presentation. I will first list (with little elaboration) many areas of his essay with which I am in agreement, followed by a discussion of the single major issue upon which we disagree.

With regard to whether Jesus literally rose from the dead, Professor Pannenberg is certainly correct that the real question is a historical one to be decided by historical research. A claim that Jesus was raised but that this belief cannot be historically researched is of little value in a discussion of this nature. More to the point, even to state such a claim entails aspects of historicity and, hence, the possibility of investigation. Further, because strong historical evidence for Jesus' Resurrection does exist, it can't be ignored for the sake of convenience or even in the name of faith. The evidence must be faced squarely, and this is one of the chief shortcomings of attempts to ignore the facts, as is frequently encountered in existential theologies. Facts just don't disappear and not only do they not exclude faith, they are actually the foundation for a faith commitment.

Professor Flew stated during our debate that a priori rejections of the Resurrection were untenable. Once again, this causes us to turn to the evidence in our study of Jesus' Resurrection.

Professor Pannenberg's treatment of the early confession in 1 Corinthians 15:3ff. further reinforced the areas mentioned in the debate. Paul not only reported demonstrably early material, but either received it directly from eyewitness sources themselves or checked the material out with them. Either way, we have strong evidence for the Resurrection.

Professor Flew contends that much can happen, even in ten years, and he is correct, for there are actually cases of such misinformation. But, as reiterated by Professor Pannenberg, this is known not to be the case with earliest Christianity, because the message is earlier still and is traceable directly to the original eyewitnesses. Of course, eyewitnesses can be mistaken, but the evidence is at its strongest in its indication that this testimony was not wrong. (Professor Pannenberg also prefers a Jerusalem location for Paul's reception of the early creed but stresses that, regardless, it was verified by the eyewitnesses.) For all of these reasons, he judges Professor Flew's position as being "not very persuasive." Additionally, the apostles made the literal Resurrection their central claim and most of them died for this specific message. This combination is not, to my knowledge, duplicated in the spread of any other religious movement.

Perhaps a brief note might be made here concerning my repetition of certain themes such as this one in the debate and in the ensuing dialogue. As Professor Pannenberg noted, my "repeated emphasis" was needed because Professor Flew avoided the issues.

One insightful comment occurred in response to Professor Flew's insistence on more evidence, to which Professor Pannenberg asserts that before one asks for more evidence, one should respond to the evidence that has already been given! I believe this is exactly what occurred in the debate; Professor Flew responded to little of the evidence for the Resurrection. And if this evidence is not addressed, it does make one wonder about his earlier disavowal of an a priori rejection.

Professor Pannenberg aptly remarks that for those who endeavor to address the question of the origins of Christianity, the issue of the Resurrection cannot be ignored. To ask how the church got started is to inquire into the nature of the earliest Resurrection claims. Therefore, when pursuing this subject we are reminded that "it becomes logically impossible to suspend judgment." One is forced to ask questions concerning the nature of the historical evidence.

Personally, I believe that the strongest argument for the historicity of Jesus' Resurrection is a case which can be based on historical facts that are accepted by virtually all scholars who investigate the subject —believers and skeptics alike. I outlined such an argument in the debate.[1] Professor Pannenberg not only agrees that such is a strong argument for the Resurrection, but points out that Professor Flew also admitted the basis for these knowable historical facts. If the Resurrection can be shown to follow from such data (and I believe that it can), we have an exceptionally powerful case for this event.

It should be noted here that although Professor Pannenberg doubts that a case for the Resurrection can be based on only the four core historical facts enumerated in my presentation, and although he is surely correct that all of the data should be utilized in such an apologetic, two items should be noted. First, the choice of just these four such facts is admittedly a fairly arbitrary one (as originally mentioned on the night of the debate), but I did it to emphasize that even when using only a portion of the evidence, a brief case can be made for the Resurrection. Besides, for purposes of arguing for this event, the fewer number of facts utilized would presumably gain a greater degree of acceptance among skeptics. Incidentally, these four facts have a much wider range than one might think, as illustrated by their applicability to the naturalistic theories, their providing major evidences, and doing both with a minimum of material, as I pointed out. So although the case rests on the entire arsenal of facts, I still believe that these four can present a brief but valid argument for the Resurrection.

Second, I specifically stated in my debate presentation that if it is thought that these four are too brief, one only needs to utilize the twelve facts that I had already delineated. The resulting apologetic for the Resurrection would remain, resting on an even broader foundation. And on this last point concerning the twelve facts, Professor Pannenberg points out his agreement.

One important application of the known historical facts concerns the subject of apparent discrepancies in the Gospel Resurrection narratives. This point is frequently missed, but because each of these accepted facts is established by historical and critical procedures and is therefore willingly recognized as historical by virtually all scholars who study this subject, and because these facts are not the ones that are challenged by disputed passages anyway, the mere presence of these apparent discrepancies does not affect this apologetic for Jesus' Resurrection, as I pointed out in my opening essay during the debate. In a strict sense, then, problems such as Professor Flew attempted to raise in his opening speech are irrelevant to our specific topic. Professor Pannenberg again notes his agreement with my assessment here.

In an important portion of his response, which has a bearing on our later discussion, Professor Pannenberg explains that he thinks the evidence additionally favors the historical fact of the empty tomb. Some of the corroboration that he lists includes Paul's implication of the empty tomb in his report of the Gospel (given the first-century Jewish understanding of the resurrection of the body), enemies of Christianity who admitted the empty tomb (although they differ on the cause), the restraint in reporting exercised by the Gospel accounts, and the fact that women are cited as the first witnesses.

For Professor Pannenberg, one significant result of the historicity of the empty tomb is that it has a bearing on the nature of Jesus' Resurrection body. When the empty tomb is utilized together with the Resurrection appearances (and they should not be treated independently), "one is pushed to literal conception of Resurrection." This issue is a crucial one and will be pursued in the next section.

During the debate Professor Flew suggested that the concept of a "spiritual body" was a contradiction. Professor Pannenberg rightly responds that this position misunderstands Paul's usage of the phrase and shows that, although we do not know many of the details, both terms are full of meaning without any contradiction whatsoever. The resurrected believer is not a vacuum, ghost, or mist, but has a new body that is more closely linked with God. The term *spiritual* by no means denotes an unreal entity, but is an adjective describing the believer's transformed body.

An important and related question to that of Jesus' Resurrection is the meaning of this unique event. Although this query actually gets us beyond the confines of our topic, strictly speaking, the subject did come up in our debate. There I briefly pointed out how the evidence indicates that the Resurrection confirms the message of Jesus, especially with regard to the kingdom of God. Professor Pannenberg apparently agrees with this assessment, which further distinguishes his position from that of Professor Flew.

Professor Pannenberg asks a question that appears to serve as a conclusion for his response. After having already granted Professor Flew that a miracle requires greater evidence to establish its occurrence than ordinary events do, he goes on to ask whether Jesus' Resurrection is attested to by that kind of evidence. Here Professor Pannenberg points out that although there is outstanding evidence for this event, humanity realizes that the dead do not ordinarily leave their graves in transformed bodies, even in exceptional cases. So what can be concluded about the Resurrection?

Having posed this question, Professor Pannenberg proceeds to delineate once again his major problem with Professor Flew's position. In spite of the initial compliment given to Professor Flew's stated rejection of a priori dismissals of miracles, Professor Pannenberg holds that just such an a priori rejection has occurred in the debate. This stance is chiefly indicated by Professor Flew's refusal to enter into very much serious discussion of the actual evidence for the Resurrection of Jesus. Therefore it is judged that Professor Flew falls prey to his own critique by not dealing with the historical facts.

A further problem for skeptics, as Professor Pannenberg agrees, is the failure of naturalistic theories to account for the facts. These skeptical attempts fail to explain the evidence "in even a half-way satisfactory form." It is added that "excessive criticism" has actually produced reports that are more incredible than the Gospel narratives themselves, hence a further indication of the bankruptcy of skepticism on this matter.

Early in his response, Professor Pannenberg agreed that historical procedures must be based on the "customary rules of regular occurrences" except in cases where such a rule does not properly account for the facts. The acceptance of the belief that all events must be analogically related to former occurrences, sometimes referred to as Troeltsch's principle of analogy, further brings to mind the point presented in the debate by Professor Flew. And again, the question is whether the Resurrection may be such a rare instance of exception.

Professor Pannenberg's answer to this query is that there are "superior reasons" for holding that Jesus was literally raised from the dead. As a result, "the risen Lord himself is a living reality." Although there will always be debate concerning the Resurrection, there will come a day in the kingdom of God when the dead will rise and no one will deny any longer that Jesus rose and is alive.

So not only is the Resurrection said to be verifiable because of its strong historical basis, but believers may look to the future kingdom of God as the time when all persons will assuredly know that Jesus was raised from the dead. This last, very intriguing assertion is certainly reminiscent of the notion of "eschatological verification" popularized by John Hick and others.[2] But it should be noted here that Professor Pannenberg is not content to say that the reality of the future kingdom is made known by faith alone or that the empirical verification at that time is all we currently have as evidence. Rather, the future revelation of God's kingdom is a fully arrived extenuation of the Resurrection of Jesus, which is a historically evidenced event in humanity's past. Therefore, historical verification of the past will be combined with eschatological verification in the future.

I found myself in substantial agreement with Professor Pannenberg's position on the Resurrection as expressed in his response to our debate. We must come to grips not only with the facts surrounding the death and Resurrection of Jesus, but also with the significance of this event for twentieth-century humanity.

As already mentioned, there is a single major area of disagreement between Professor Pannenberg and myself as expressed in his response. This concerns the form of Jesus' appearances. It is Professor Pannenberg's conviction that "Paul's experience of the risen Jesus cannot have been altogether different from the appearances that occurred to Peter, James, and the other apostles." And because the Gospels report Jesus' appearances "in a much more earthly fashion," indicative of increasing apologetic formation, Professor Pannenberg prefers the sort of experiences that Paul observed on the road to Damascus. So although the Gospels are "not . . . historically worthless" and "they certainly include valid points of historical information," they are said to be not as reliable as I intimate in the debate.

Especially because this is such a crucial issue in contemporary discussions of the Resurrection, and also because it came up earlier in the debate with Professor Flew, I will attempt to outline a brief case for bodily Resurrection appearances of Jesus as presented in the Gospels that does not neglect Paul's appearance either. But it must be specifically noted that, although this portion of the response appears in the section pertaining to Professor Pannenberg, it is by no means directed entirely to him. Indeed, he is even in agreement with some of the following points. Rather, I am responding to the question in general, portions of which, however, do pertain especially to his position. Three specific points should be made here.

First, it is the view of many critical scholars that the Gospels and Acts contain not only eyewitness testimony, but that apostolic authority is a major source behind each of these books.[3] The details cannot be argued here in the proper context of this response, but suffice it to say that a perhaps surprising number of critical scholars support the thesis that Mark,[4] Luke and Acts,[5] Matthew,[6] and even John[7] contain important amounts of such apostolic data.

This conclusion is certainly an important one in terms of the question of Jesus' Resurrection appearances.[8] If there is any significant amount of eyewitness testimony in any of the Gospels, one would suspect that the accounts of the death and Resurrection of Jesus would be the crucial point for such testimony, because it is the central focus of the New Testament. In other words, if any of the Gospels attempted to include any eyewitness testimony, what subject would be a more likely candidate than the content of the Gospel?

Although it is frequently claimed that the Gospels reflect a later period featuring the growth of legend in the interests of apologetics, one problem for such a claim is precisely the presence of this eyewitness testimony. This is not to say that eyewitness testimony guarantees complete accuracy in ancient (or modern) documents, for such is simply not the case. But it must likewise be recognized that neither do legendary developments nullify a text.

When applied to the Gospels, we must also be reminded that although the date of their composition is later than Paul's Epistle to the Corinthians, it is not a significant amount of time after the original events. We may get so used to thinking of the Gospels as late testimony that we forget that they follow the events in question by only thirty-five to sixty-five years.

It is here that the testimonies of ancient historians such as Michael Grant and A. N. Sherwin-White are so important. As already pointed out in the dialogues, these scholars assert that the Gospels and Acts are good sources of historical facts. For example, Sherwin-White utilizes Herodotus' history as an effort that parallels the writing of the Gospels in that this Greek historian also wrote about one or two generations after the events that he describes, utilizing oral tradition as his source, and, in addition, wrote with enthusiasm and commitment, using recorded events as a vehicle to express moral and religious ideas. And yet much history can be successfully extracted from Herodotus' record.

Sherwin-White points out that Herodotus provides a test case for the rapidity with which legend can take over a text, and he concludes that "the tests suggest that even two generations are too short a time span to allow the mythical tendency to prevail over the hard historic core of the oral tradition."[9] The Gospels and Acts present at least as good a basis for history.[10] And although some will protest that ancient historians and the Gospel authors belong to different kinds of literature, Sherwin-White and Grant point out that ancient historians frequently do parallel the Gospels in intent and methodology, so the strict separation cannot be maintained. Further, much of the Gospels are verified by independent examination and the facts can be separated from theologizing anyway.[11]

So although it is true that in some cases legend has crept into religious teaching quickly,[12] ancient historians such as Sherwin-White and Grant point out that the issue is not whether legend has crept in at some point, because such does not destroy the knowledge of the "historical core of the oral tradition."[13]

And such a conclusion is what we find when we move to the Gospel accounts of the Resurrection. As mentioned in my initial debate essay, C. H. Dodd drew some careful conclusions after a specialized study of the Gospel narratives of the Resurrection appearances. He pointed out that these narratives can be divided into "concise" reports and "tales." The first group consists of appearances that are reported without much elaboration and are apparently drawn directly from the earlier and more corporate oral traditions. The second group consists of unformed or more "free" oral traditions. The former group presumably has a greater claim to historicity, but Dodd stresses that the "tales" are not thereby to be disregarded in a study of the actual appearances of Jesus.

Nonetheless, Matthew 28:8–10, 16–20, John 20:19–21, and, to a lesser extent, Luke 24:36–39 are identified as concise accounts based on more formalized tradition. As such, these Gospel Resurrection narratives can provide especially good information, as can early traditions such as 1 Corinthians 15:3ff., concerning the original appearances to the apostles.[14]

Therefore, strong evidence indicates that the Gospel Resurrection narratives contain reliable testimony concerning Jesus' appearances to his disciples. The converging evidence from eyewitness and apostolic testimony in the Gospels, the evidence against legends changing the essence of the original reports, and the fact that early and authoritative traditions exist in these narratives all point strongly to this conclusion. Additionally, the centrality of the Gospel message and the emphasis on the accurate reporting of it, as well as the presence of largely independent Resurrection narratives from various communities make this conclusion all the more noteworthy when it is remembered that the Gospels are unanimous in their claim that Jesus rose and appeared bodily (although definitely with new powers). Thus whatever eyewitness and apostolic reports are contained in the Gospels, all agree on the bodily appearances of the risen Jesus. This is quite a string of evidence, which I think would be difficult to disallow.

A second indication of the bodily appearances of Jesus is the facticity of the empty tomb, concerning which Professor Pannenberg (along with many other scholars) has made it clear that he also accepts. Again, all four Gospels teach the empty tomb, and I think that Professor

Pannenberg is correct that Paul implies it in 1 Corinthians 15:3–4. There are many noteworthy arguments for the empty tomb,[15] but these will not be listed here, chiefly because none of the three respondents questioned it (and two of them explicitly accepted its historicity).

But it would appear that there are at least a couple of connections between the empty tomb and a bodily Resurrection of Jesus. The obvious relation is that Jesus' body was buried and later it was his body that was gone from the tomb. It is logically possible that the transformation was from a physical body to a glorified spirit-being. Yet it appears that because the evidence indicates a Resurrection, the empty tomb would more consistently point to the raising of a more physical body, especially because a spirit-being could presumably be immortal with a dead body remaining in its original condition in the tomb. Thus the fact that the tomb was vacated is an indication that whatever happened probably occurred to the body. Additionally, in first-century Palestinian belief, the view of the Resurrection of the body was apparently the predominant one.[16] It is difficult to conceive of first-century Jews teaching an empty tomb and resurrected Jesus without at the same time referring to the body of Jesus.

Professor Pannenberg apparently accepts this basic twofold reasoning as well, but then draws back from any concept of Jesus' Resurrection body such as that presented in the Gospels. Professor Pannenberg even states in his response that

the judgment concerning the kind of reality that occurred with the appearances cannot be independent of the question of what happened to the tomb. . . . If one accepts the empty-tomb tradition, one is pushed to a literal conception of Resurrection.

Now it is possible to conceive of a Resurrection body that is not the general one portrayed in the Gospels, but it appears to me to be counterproductive to do so once one has recognized the importance of both the empty tomb and the predominant Jewish view of resurrection of the body. These arguments seem to strongly favor a picture like the one presented in the Gospel narrative—literal, bodily appearances including the presence of some changes.

A third consideration for a bodily Resurrection concerns Paul's teaching in 1 Corinthians 15. It is commonly assumed that Paul talks about a much less corporeal Resurrection body, as indicated by his inclusion of his appearance with the others (verses 3–8), which is said to mean that Paul believed that Jesus appeared to him in the same sort of body as witnessed by the others, plus his teaching on the "spiritual body" (verses 35–49) and his statement that "flesh and blood" cannot inherit incorruption (verse 50).

Initially we should investigate the claim made by some that the Resurrection appearance to Paul was only an objective vision—a real but inward revelation known to no one but the recipient.[17] One major (and I think a rather decisive) problem with this position is its tendency to utilize the three reports in Acts (9:1–9, 22:6–11, and 26:12–18) where they fit the hypothesis and to disregard the reports where they do not.

For example, to speak of Paul's experience at all generally requires at least some reference to the Acts accounts, yet these same accounts, although showing some signs of such an objective visionary description, inform us that the overall experience cannot be characterized as such. In at least three facets of the reports we are told that the appearance measurably affected the participants. Both Paul and his companions heard a voice, although the men with Paul didn't understand the message (Acts 9:7, 22:9).[18] Both also saw the extraordinary light from heaven (Acts 22:9), which even resulted in the entire group falling to the ground (Acts 26:13–14). And Paul himself was physically blinded for three days after the experience (Acts 9:8–9, 22:11).

Of course, one can attempt to explain away physical effects such as the sound of the voice, the light, and the blinding, but it appears like a rejection based on one's own presuppositions when the objective elements are dismissed but the subjective ones are retained. To utilize the texts in Acts, as most scholars appear to desire, would seem to indicate some objective physical effects.

One related point recognized by most scholars is that Paul distinguished between the Resurrection appearance to him and other visions that he received. This is another indication of the fact that his appearance was not merely a vision, but had effects in reality. This, Craig notes, is a crucial issue. Because visions are generally defined as private revelations, and because Paul's appearance was not a vision (as Paul makes clear) then neither was his experience a private manifestation only.[19]

Now it should be carefully noted that this discussion of Paul's experience so far should not, in general, be taken as a criticism of Professor Pannenberg's position, for such a charge would be mistaken. He also believes that the Resurrection appearances had real effects and are not to be construed as inward private visions without veridicality.[20]

But from this point on we differ. For instance, even Professor Pannenberg argues that the Acts account of Paul's experience is more trustworthy than the accounts of Jesus' Resurrection body in Luke 24 and Acts 1. This helps to illustrate not only my point that most critical scholars utilize the three Acts accounts that report Paul's conversion, but also illustrates my earlier assertion concerning choosing some passages and rejecting others. Why prefer Paul's accounts and reject the nature of the appearances to the other apostles reported in the same book (Acts 1)? Luke 1:1-4 asserts that eyewitness testimony was a major source of information. If this is rejected, what about Paul's conversion narratives? Actually, both are based on good sources. Paul's testimony and the word of other eyewitnesses are present, as confirmed by historical and archaeological data previously mentioned.

On a more important issue, Professor Pannenberg (agreeing with Professor Flew) believes that the appearances to the disciples were similar to Paul's experience. But there is strong evidence that no such identification should be made. (1) In 1 Corinthians 15:8 Paul specifically notes a temporal difference between his experience and those of the other apostles with the words " ἔσχατον δὲ πάντων ὡσπερεὶ τῷ ἐκτρώματι ὤφθη κἀμοί." He states that the appearance to him was "aborted" (ἐκτρώματι) and differed at least in this respect. Because Paul specifically notes this point of temporal variation, it remains an open question as to whether he means to imply that the type of appearance was also different. But Paul by no means asserts that all the appearances were the same. To argue otherwise is simply an argument from silence. In fact, it is the reality of the appearances that concerns Paul here, not their mode, for what his list demands is that

Jesus literally appeared to certain witnesses. An anatomical study is not the point of Paul's teaching in his citing of the early creed.

Professor Pannenberg argues in his response that because Paul was confirmed by the Jerusalem apostles, their experiences must have been similar. This is an unusual point. The apostles' confirmation specifically applied to the facticity of the Gospel, not to the comparative anatomy of the Resurrection appearances. Besides, to argue that the apostles thereby acknowledged that the type of experience witnessed by Paul was normative begs the question. Isn't it possible that Paul knew of corporeal appearances like those described in the Gospels but was at ease with them (or the apostles were at ease with Paul's accounts in spite of the differences)? Incidentally, Luke had no problem recording both types of appearances (see following text). The fact that Luke and Acts record both the appearances to the apostles and to Paul without any hint of conflict is stronger evidence than the presumed approval of the apostles toward Paul on the subject of the anatomy of Jesus' Resurrection body when we have no evidence that the nature of the appearances was the crucial issue.

(2) One of Paul's personal desires appears to be to remind his readers that he was a true apostle (vv. 9–10). Accordingly, Paul's claim to apostleship could have influenced him to add his appearance to the list —after all, he had really seen the Lord. And once again, the issue for Paul is who had seen the Lord, not the physicality of the Lord's body.

(3) It used to be repeated frequently (and sometimes still is) that Paul's choice of ὁράω indicates that he was speaking of visionary experiences for everyone. But it should be noted that ὁράω does not specify either bodily or visionary sight.[21] In fact, the word is utilized even more frequently in the New Testament with regard to physical sight. Both Luke and John use ὁράω to describe Jesus' appearances to the disciples in their Resurrection narratives,[22] which points out the futility of holding that ὁράω must indicate some spiritual vision.

(4) For those who believe that the evidence favors Luke as both the companion of Paul and the author of the third Gospel and Acts, it should also be added that Luke, who records the most details about Paul's experience with the Lord, also reports the bodily appearances of Jesus to his disciples. Apparently Luke, although aware of both kinds

of experience, saw no problem with recording both, believing them to be an accurate account of what actually happened. Luke additionally identifies Paul's teaching on the resurrection of the body with the literal form of that doctrine held by the Pharisees (Acts 23:6). The point here is that Paul's including himself in the early list of Resurrection appearances proves nothing about whether he thought that his experience was of the same kind as that of the other apostles. Although he recognized a temporal difference and although he wished to be recognized as an apostle, these and other considerations establish that Paul neither addressed nor answered the question as to whether he included his appearance with the others because they were of the same type. The word ὁράω is too general to assist us here. Luke's information is helpful, especially because he was Paul's companion and biographer, but the issue is still open. John A. T. Robinson addresses this question as follows:

The only real evidence for this thesis . . . is that Paul regarded all the other appearances as conforming to the pattern of his own vision on the Damascus Road. But there is little basis for such a deduction. So far from regarding his own vision as normative, he marvels at his right to include it in the series at all. Paul, in fact, says nothing about the manner of the appearances. . . . In the gospel records it is arbitrary to arrange the appearances in order of increasing materialization.[23]

But many researchers would argue that Paul settles the issue in 1 Corinthians 15:35–58, especially in verses 44–45 and 50. A debate response does not lend itself to in-depth exegesis, but a few comments are in order. In 1 Corinthians 15:44–45 Paul states that believers will be given "spiritual bodies" and then refers to Jesus as a "life-giving spirit." We have already seen that the composition of Jesus' Resurrection body is not addressed by Paul in the earlier list of appearances that he relates. Neither can his own experience be referred to as an internal vision without outward effects. Therefore we have no conceptual or contextual basis for concluding that Paul dismisses a bodily Resurrection, and neither do verses 35–58 supply such a teaching. As Craig insists:

For Paul ψυχή and πνεῦμα are not substances out of which bodies are made, but dominating principles by which bodies are directed. Virtually every modern commentator agrees on this point: Paul is not talking about a rarefied body made out of spirit or ether; he means a body under the lordship and direction of God's Spirit.[24]

With regard to verse 45, is Jesus specifically being called a spirit? We must answer in the negative or be prepared to do violence to both the text and Paul's doctrine of anthropology, for if this verse means that Jesus is a bodiless spirit, then, in its own textual contrast, Adam was a bodiless soul. This teaching would also violate Jewish anthropology. Again, Paul is addressing not the composition of the Resurrection body but its source of power.

Even though Murray J. Harris believes that Jesus' "essential state was one of invisibility and therefore immateriality,"[25] he agrees that 1 Corinthians 15:44–45 does not teach that Jesus was a spirit:

However, the Resurrection did not convert Jesus into "pure spirit." . . . In his resurrection Jesus is "life-giving spirit" (I Cor. 15:45) in the sense that his is a form of corporeality in which the spirit is supreme.[26]

In 1 Corinthians 15:50, Paul likewise is not discussing Jesus' anatomy. The phrase "flesh and blood" is widely used in Semitic idiom, and appears both in Paul and in other books of the New Testament.[27] It means that mortal human bodies cannot experience immortality; our bodies cannot enter eternal life as they are presently. Hence, a transforming change is needed. Again Craig comments that "virtually all modern commentators agree that these expressions have nothing to do with substantiality or anatomy."[28] Harris agrees: "We cannot, as frail mortals, ever inherit God's kingdom nor can what is perishable inherit what is imperishable (v. 50)."[29] And later: "It is impossible for anything that is liable to corruption to inherit an incorruptible order (v. 50)."[30] In this case the second half of verse 50 complements and explains the first half. The point is that believers must be changed before they can enter the kingdom of God and experience eternal life. Paul uses a Semitic idiom to point out the perishability of our mortal bodies; Resurrection anatomy is just not the point.

Therefore there is no need to take Paul's doctrine as disagreeing with the teaching in the Gospels at all. Again, John A. T. Robinson remarks after a comparison of the Gospel teachings with that of Paul:

All the appearances, in fact, depict the same phenomenon, of a body identical yet changed, transcending the limitations of the flesh yet capable of manifesting itself within the order of the flesh. We may describe this as a "spiritual" (I Cor. 15:44) or "glorified" (cf. I Cor. 15:43; Phil. 3:21) body . . . so long as we do not import into these phrases any opposition to the physical as such.[31]

An additional point here, as implied by Robinson, concerns the nature of the body in New Testament thought. It was chiefly construed in a holistic sense, incorporating body and immaterial portion.[32] This would also militate against any noncorporeal interpretation of Jesus' Resurrection body by Paul or others.

So even if one does not concede that Paul was in agreement with the Gospel authors on the nature of Jesus' Resurrection body, neither can one assert that Paul assumed that all the appearances of Jesus were of the same nature. This is a conclusion which simply proceeds beyond the evidence. In fact, Paul does not even address the issue of the anatomy of the Resurrection body, except to say that physical bodies must be transformed into spiritual bodies. On this point the Gospels agree. Professor Pannenberg, in his response, also recognized the Gospel's insistence on the transformed body of Jesus.

Again, in all fairness to Professor Pannenberg, he agrees with this presentation at several points and so this section should not be construed as a response to him only. And, of course, Professor Pannenberg and I agree on the most important single fact in this debate, the literal Resurrection of Jesus. But we do disagree most significantly on the nature of Jesus' Resurrection appearances and the part that the Gospels play in the discussion. I have even greater disagreements on these issues with Professors Flew and Hartshorne. And it is here that I believe that the strong evidence in favor of the historicity of the Gospels and the empty tomb (including its significance) provide compelling facts in favor of a corporeal Resurrection of Jesus' body, although in a transformed state. Paul's teaching, on the other hand, does not militate against these conclusions. The Gospels stress the corporeal nature of Jesus' body and Paul emphasizes its transformed nature. But there is no contradiction here. The Gospels certainly recognize the quality of transformation and Paul does not deny the element of a bodily Resurrection.

PROFESSOR CHARLES HARTSHORNE

The response by Professor Hartshorne is divided into two general categories—immortality of the soul and the Resurrection of Jesus. I will treat them in reverse order.

Two preliminary issues must be addressed. First, although Professor Hartshorne makes it clear that he is a theist (based on six arguments, as he indicates), he begins by stating that he still agrees somewhat with Hume's teaching that whenever a miracle is reported, the report is likely to be in error. Various problems with Hume's thesis have been pointed out throughout this dialogue (especially in my opening debate essay) and these will not be repeated here. Even Professors Flew and Hartshorne have stated some areas of disagreement with Hume.

The chief point to be made here is that Professor Hartshorne's statement is basically correct. It is likely that most miracle claims are incorrect. But, unless one is prepared to retreat in an a priori manner, one cannot use this maneuver to avoid dealing with evidence in a specific case. It has been shown that there is superior evidence for Jesus' Resurrection and to simply say that most miracle claims are mistaken does not disintegrate that evidence. So although the majority of miracle claims may even be proven false upon investigation, this cannot be assumed without such a study. And because the evidence for the Resurrection remains after such a study, it cannot be disposed of by judgments based on other miracle claims.

Especially because Professor Hartshorne specifically remarks that he cannot explain away the evidence for the Resurrection (and Professor Flew didn't do so), it is intellectually perilous not to deal specifically with it; to merely counter that it is more likely that miracle claims are false does not suffice. If we think we know that no miracle could ever occur and we don't seriously view the evidence, then we are making an a priori objection. But if miracles are at least possible, then we ought to be willing to deal with the evidence in a serious manner. As Professor

Pannenberg remarks, to claim that we need more evidence, as Professor Flew did, assumes that the large amount already given has been accounted for in an adequate manner, which was not done. And to say there are discrepancies in the text misses the present argument by a wide margin because the case for the Resurrection that was presented here was based solely on historical data that are recognized as facts by virtually all scholars who deal with the subject. In other words, the case is made without using the material that Professor Flew or others question.

Second, Professor Hartshorne insists that faith ought not be based on historical facts and that historical facts are not even important in this context. And yet, if faith is not based on facts, what distinguishes this view from fideism? Yet I assume that Professor Hartshorne is not a fideist, because he notes several major reasons for his faith. But if he believes when there are rational reasons, is it inconceivable that faith can also be exercised when there are historical reasons?

In actuality there is no necessity that delimits faith or indicates that it must be kept separate from historical facts. We regularly make decisions based on the facts and there is no reason that such should not be the case in theological matters as well. And it makes sense that when eternal consequences are at stake, one be more sure of the grounds of belief. Without a factual basis, how can we know if our faith is placed in the correct object? Professor Hartshorne wouldn't take the view that he does unless he believed it was sound. That we debate this is a further indication of the need for epistemic warrant.

So if the Gospel claims are factual, the exercise of faith is a natural consequence. In fact, I would assert that faith is practically impossible without some factual basis. To assert otherwise involves rational disputation and is self-defeating. Besides, Christianity does not advocate placing faith in facts so much as in the person whom the facts concern. But the facts are nonetheless present, which brings us back to the issue of Jesus' Resurrection.

One interesting facet of Professor Hartshorne's response is that although he (like Professor Flew) avoids proposing a naturalistic theory to account for the facts, he does hint at a few options. His suggestion that the swoon theory is a possibility (although Professor Hartshorne clearly declares neutrality) is interesting in light of the present state of this issue. I treated this issue briefly in the question and answer period, pointing out that the nature of crucifixion as death by asphyxiation (confirmed by both medical science and archaeology), the nature of the chest wound and its confirmation of death (verified by both medical science and Roman history), and any corroboration from the Shroud of Turin (because the man is assuredly dead, including rigor mortis) all demonstrate the futility of such a hypothesis. But both historically and logically, the chief reason for the failure of the swoon theory is David Strauss's trenchant criticism that even by its own criteria, this view cannot explain virtually any of the relevant historical facts. If Jesus did not die, the sequence of events between the Cross and the post-Cross appearances is so fantastic as to cause doubt in the most stringent of critics. But even beyond credulity are the appearances themselves. A nearly dead, grievously wounded Jesus would not convince the disciples that he had been raised and in a new, transformed body, as well![33] To construe the appearances otherwise ignores the critically known historical facts.[34]

Therefore it is no surprise that the swoon theory was rejected long ago by almost every critic who addressed this issue. Schweitzer includes no proponents of this hypothesis after 1840.[35] By the turn of the century, Eduard Riggenbach and James Orr referred to it as no more than a historical curiosity.[36] More examples are readily available, but even Professor Flew called this thesis "rubbish" during our dialogue, for it does not account for the facts.

Professor Hartshorne also intimates that the variety of miraculous claims in the world religions obscures the Resurrection accounts in the New Testament. What he (correctly) doesn't assert is the older view that Christianity was inspired by the ancient mystery religions.[37] But his comparison nonetheless contains several difficulties.

For example, Professor Hartshorne asserts, "I do not feel that I can choose among such accounts." But while merely throwing one's hands up in question might appear to be an initial response to apparent obscurities in ancient history, such practice flies in the face of the discipline of history. As Sherwin-White and Grant point out, historians regularly sift through legend and discern fact. And with ancient history, this may be the chief methodology.[38] So although Professor Hartshorne's approach may seem to be a convenient way out, it does not accord with historical methodology.

Another problem with this approach is that it uncritically lumps together accounts of persons such as Buddha (to utilize Professor Hartshorne's example), whose exploits were largely reported one to three centuries after his death, with the earliest evidence for Jesus' Resurrection, which dates from directly after the event. Such methodology runs the risk of rejecting historical fact by confusing it with legend. This is similar to the problem spoken of previously regarding Hume. Just because some ancient accounts may be legendary (in this case, miracles attributed to Buddha are certainly suspect), we ought not ignore good evidence for other events such as the Resurrection.

Before leaving the subject of Jesus' Resurrection, a few last points should be noted. Professor Hartshorne remarks during his response that although there is empirical evidence for Jesus' life, "empirical evidence . . . is not sufficient for all our cognitive needs." I would remark here that although such evidence may not satisfy all our wishes, the very presence of such a quality type of corroboration is significant for a study of Jesus' life. Later he asserts, "I can neither explain away the evidences to which Habermas appeals, nor can I simply agree with Flew's or Hume's positions." After granting some historical (empirical) evidence for Jesus earlier, I find this statement to be quite positive. Because Professor Hartshorne identifies himself as one whose "metaphysical bias is against resurrections," admitting that he couldn't explain away the evidence for Jesus' Resurrection is encouraging. Perhaps it is a frank statement and a witness from an honest skeptic to the strong evidence for this event.

The other major topic discussed by Professor Hartshorne in his response is the subject of the immortality of the soul, which, in its personal form, he rejects. He states that there is no immortality except "objective immortality" as taught by Whitehead. Yet he appears to be willing to keep the subject open, saying that any other form of life after death must be left up to God. But he adds that if we someday experience personal life after death, we won't be able to prove that it is immortal life. Providing a few reasons for his position, he asserts that personal immortality distorts the ideas of God, mind, and consciousness. In particular, to want to live forever is akin to wishing one were God. In one of his recent works, we are similarly told that personal immortality amounts to either being bored for eternity or the desire to be God.[39] In contrast, objective immortality teaches that one's life experience is given everlasting status by God in the sense that one is loved and remembered by God forever, although no personal consciousness remains.

I think that this view is not in accord with the facts, because life after death is one of the strongest attested facets of natural theology. There are many arguments for life after death,[40] two of which will be mentioned here. First, the evidence reveals that Jesus was raised from the dead, which is not only a specific case of life after death given by example, but Jesus' teachings on the subject (including personal immortality) would also be given credence by his Resurrection (as outlined in my debate rebuttal).[41]

Second, scientific study of the near-death experience has proceeded well beyond some of the more popular works of a decade ago and has produced reputable, statistical studies of this phenomena. In fact, numerous veridical experiences have not only been corroborated, but have occurred while the person was clinically dead (including several cases where there was a flat EEG reading).

In other words, in some cases a person viewed other individuals, events, or circumstances that would not normally have been in the range of their sense experience and correctly reported numerous details even though they were clinically dead or even while they had flat EEG readings. Some recent experiments were completed with regard to these reports, including some rather ingenious controls, which concluded that at least some of these persons did report facts that they could not have known by any natural means and did so while clinically dead.

The strongest cases are those where there was a combination of empirically observed and corroborated data (especially when such was not normally observable given the location of the person) in the presence of clinical death (including flat EEG readings in several cases). Although irreversible death did not occur in these instances, these observations are unexplained in known natural terms, and because clinical death (and sometimes brain inactivity) had already occurred, we have strong evidence at least for minimalistic life after death, because personal consciousness has been evidenced beyond the initial stages of death. The scientific controls add to this case.[42]

The objection that the consciousness of these individuals is still a result of interaction with the central nervous system is opposed by the cases of brain inactivity in the presence of corroborative experiences. But even the clinical death cases by themselves strongly militate against this thesis when viewed along with the verified perceptions of data beyond the person's senses. The common objections of hallucinations or physical, mental, or drug-related conditions all fall prey to the veridical experiences just mentioned, because these reports are thereby objectively verified. Even Professor Flew was impressed with this evidence and, in a discussion with this writer, pointed out that it is potentially the best recent evidence for life after death.[43]

What about Professor Hartshorne's objections? Does life after death distort concepts of the mind and consciousness? Although he provides no details, I can only conclude that such claimed distortions would be a problem for his view, not for one that accords with the data (although we only mentioned two evidences and in a cursory manner). If the facts confirm personal life after death, it would not distort that concept of the mind that is thereby established.

Can we ever know that immortality is true and that life after death is extended to eternity? I think that the teachings of Jesus, confirmed by his Resurrection, are the best indication of this fact.[44] At any rate, the evidence of life after death itself still militates against Professor Hartshorne's position.

Is immortality either boring or a quest for omniscience? This charge is a false dilemma, and is a classic, textbook case of the black-white informal fallacy of logic. These are far from being the only options. In fact, the concept of heaven is quite meaningful.[45] But I can't share Professor Hartshorne's enthusiasm for the permanent cherishing by God which, as he says, gives lasting status to each of us even though we no longer experience consciousness. I find this to be as undesirable as it is unfounded in fact.

Although Professor Hartshorne ends his essay with the words, "My metaphysical bias is against resurrections," I would hope that metaphysics would not be formulated in opposition to the historical facts. The evidence favors the Resurrection of Jesus, and because Professor Hartshorne has stated that he cannot explain away these evidences, it would appear that a "metaphysical bias" should not stand in the way of our conclusion of facticity.

In light of the evidence for the Resurrection of Jesus, we have a strong foundation not only for the event itself, but also for the personal immortality of persons who commit their lives to Jesus in view of his message. And once again, this commitment is a decision based on the facts of the Gospel, described by Paul in 1 Corinthians 15:3–4 as the atoning death, burial, and Resurrection of Christ.

PROFESSOR JAMES I. PACKER

The response by Professor Packer begins as an eloquent exposition of the importance of the Resurrection of Jesus. It is correct that this event both provides a factual basis for the great doctrines of Christianity and separates it from the rest of the world's religions. The Resurrection is the capstone of the Gospel message that Jesus Christ died for the sins of the world, was buried, and rose again from the dead (1 Corinthians 15:3–4). A faith commitment to the Jesus of this message brings eternal life.

But as Paul also tells us, this event distinguishes between Christianity and other philosophies and belief systems. He even states that if Jesus had not been raised from the dead, thereby guaranteeing the believer's Resurrection, then he or she might as well live life simply to have a good time, for no Christian hope would remain (1 Corinthians 15:20, 32). In this case the Resurrection makes Christianity what it is, for with it Paul clings to Jesus' message; without it he asserts that this teaching should be abandoned in favor of another philosophy. It is the Resurrection of Jesus that makes all the difference. It even governs how one's present life ought to be lived.

The facticity of the Resurrection similarly gives meaning to the rest of the Gospel message, for it shows that Jesus did not die in vain. Further, this event is the prototype of the believer's eternal life. It even reveals God's approval and verification of Jesus' message, including the deity that he claimed. It provides a basis for a Christian ethic and inspires believers to an objective hope and goal for the future.[46]

But as Professor Packer notes, there are certainly scholars who attempt to have the best of both worlds—to both affirm some spiritual occurrence and to stay skeptical (including denying certain facets of the narratives that are clearly historical). And such views are often assaulted for not being skeptical enough, on the one hand, and for not affirming a historical Resurrection, on the other. Then there are those who affirm the Resurrection but not the logical consequences that proceed from it; Professor Packer's example of practitioners of New Age philosophies is applicable. The Resurrection is affirmed but not the uniqueness of the one who was raised. But it is in this combination of unique event plus unique person and claims that Jesus is best viewed. The Resurrection ought not be taken in isolation but along with the entire context of the one who is risen. It may seem to be easy to view one side of the picture or the other—the event or the person and teachings—but they cannot be separated, as I asserted in my rebuttal during the debate.

At this point a couple of questions concerning the mechanics of the debate itself must be answered. Professor Packer suggests that two other topics be included—the importance of the Resurrection in terms of such subjects as the deity of Jesus and the existence of God. He admits that the former would be outside the strict topic of historicity, but chides us for not including the latter.

With regard to the question of importance, this issue is difficult to address when one debater does not concede the chief event upon which the point rests. In other words, the Resurrection has importance because it occurred in literal history (certain existential and other theologies notwithstanding). Concerning God's existence, we were afraid that the conversation would bog down at that point and we would never get past it to even pose the question of the Resurrection. Professor Packer himself acknowledges, "There is, however, a built-in limitation: you can debate only one question at a time." So although it would have been beneficial to include the Resurrection in a theistic context, we had to limit the conversation.

With reference to what Professor Packer terms Professor Flew's "dogmatic agnosticism," here is where I believe his response was the most potent. The point is that anyone can claim to be impregnable on virtually any position if he or she chooses to deny good evidence virtually without any reasons for doing so or by taking the contrary position beyond the point that other evidence allows and by further circumscribing one's position so that it is not falsifiable under any circumstance. But, Professor Packer asserts, the question is not whether the position claims impregnability, "the . . . question is whether a stance thus defined and circumscribed can be thought of as reasonable."

Did Professor Flew make his case thusly? Professor Packer lists at least two indications that he built just such a misleading defense. First, Professor Flew took the point concerning hallucinations and extended it "beyond anything that psychologists have yet been able to observe and describe." As noted, this is certainly a hazardous maneuver for an empiricist who utilizes scientific data in the manner that Professor Flew does. ("Live by science, die by science," one might say.)

Second, Professor Flew attempted to gainsay reports from ten years after the event and to downplay firsthand reports of the Resurrection appearances of Jesus when such stand on solid, eyewitness grounds and when ten years is a short time for people to remember unusual events. Once again, although eyewitness reports can be altered, the facts militate strongly at every point against such a thesis in this case.

Is it true, however, that I did not "hammer" Professor Flew enough for not being aware of the latest state of the issue, or "for not facing evidence" and thus for rejecting the Resurrection in an a priori manner, as Professor Packer charges? Or did I "pull punches" because of politeness? I confess to preferring to make my points in a cordial manner whenever possible. We did, however, have several sharp confrontations, and I believe the record will show that there is no single issue that I stressed more than Professor Flew's unwillingness to deal with the evidences, especially with regard to the eyewitness testimony such as that manifested in the early creed in 1 Corinthians 15:3ff. My closing statement following the question and answer period was largely devoted to this very issue, charging Professor Flew with not adequately addressing the facts for the Resurrection.

What about the evidence for Jesus' Resurrection? Professor Packer compliments it except for the Shroud of Turin. But, if it is possible to judge from one paragraph, Professor Packer appears to have missed much of the relevant data concerning this artifact. Or if one paragraph is too brief to ascertain this, then at least several statements in it need to be corrected. First, one does not guess what caused the image and then utilize the first answer to guess again as to whom the cloth belongs. This is the opposite of the procedure employed, as far as I am aware, by virtually all shroud researchers who are concerned with the issue of identifying the man buried in it. Unless there are already good historical reasons for addressing the question of identity,[47] one should not then jump to the issue of the cause of the image. To argue from a strange image to Jesus in hopes of completing the puzzle is to beg the question.

Additionally, Professor Packer's contention is that the shroud "is just a tantalizing medieval oddity: no more." If he simply means that the shroud was discovered in medieval times, then its previous history needs to be discussed. On the other hand, if he means that it is a hoax, then this is something he must prove, which may be a difficult job; some of the best scientific minds have not been able to accomplish the task of showing how the shroud could be a medieval creation.[48] But certainly more will be needed than an accusation.

Professor Packer may be correct that the case for the shroud is not independent of other evidence for the Resurrection, although I have argued otherwise.[49] But I cannot agree with him that the shroud evidence "does not . . . strengthen the case for Jesus' Resurrection." Not only would I argue that the evidence provided is independent, but, regardless, it certainly strengthens the already existing historical case.

Lest I be misunderstood, I wish to make two additional points. First, as I have already affirmed many times in print (including this debate), the shroud could be disproven at some future date. As an object of scientific investigation, more data could strengthen or weaken present knowledge. Second, I also mention regularly that, of the four major sets of evidence that I have adduced for Jesus' Resurrection, the Shroud of Turin is the weakest. But this is not to say that it is not a strong argument at this time, for I believe that it is. And this conclusion is based on extensive (even if not a final) investigation.

With regard to the other evidences for Jesus' Resurrection, I believe that Professor Packer and I are in agreement. His kind words concerning the "technical excellence" of the case that I presented are appreciated, as is his comment that this case is certainly strong enough to persuade most people. He is certainly correct that Jesus' Resurrection must be anchored in "Israel's history and faith and Jesus' life and teaching," and I outlined a case in which one might proceed in that direction during my rebuttal period in the debate,[50] as Professor Packer notes. The Resurrection must be linked to a broader theistic context in order for its fullest significance to be perceived.

I appreciate his zeroing in on the "sheer impossibility" of the Resurrection faith starting and being proclaimed in Jerusalem with the body of Jesus still in the tomb. This scenario basically expanded my listing of "known facts" numbers 6–9. He is correct that this is a strong argument and it is built, as pointed out in the debate, on facts granted by virtually all scholars who study this area.

In conclusion, Professor Packer is certainly correct in his assertion that belief (which, in the biblical sense, is commitment) cannot be induced through argumentation. Faith is exercised in the Jesus of the facts, but facts alone do not necessarily lead to faith. Argument by itself does not produce believers. Yet debate can be helpful in clarifying issues and bringing arguments to light. Discourse is useful in its own right, as Professor Packer notes.

In our case, the topic could hardly be a more important one for contemporary religious thought. Professor Flew pointed out its importance, both theoretically and practically. As an example, Professor Flew asserted further that it could be "the best, if not the only, reason for accepting that Jesus is the God of Abraham, Isaac, and Israel." Although I don't think it is the only evidence for Christian theism (I believe there are literally many), I do agree that it is the best argument for Jesus' deity. And I end where I began, in differing with Professor Flew in that I think that the evidence is overwhelming in favor of the Resurrection, which, accordingly, would verify Jesus' claims to deity and serve as a call to the people of the world to commit their lives to him. Our eternal destiny hangs in the balance.

NOTES

1. For a more in depth treatment, see Gary Habermas, *Ancient Evidence for the Life of Jesus: Historical Records of His Death and Resurrection, op. cit.* (Nashville: Nelson, 1984), "Primary Sources: Creeds and Facts."

2. Cf. John Hick, "Theology and Verification," *Theology Today* 17 (April 1960).

3. Of the five books being considered, Matthew is perhaps the one with the least apostolic acclaim among critical scholars. Mark, Luke, John, and Acts are well attested to in this regard. (See footnotes 4–7 that follow.)

4. C. E. B. Cranfield, *The Gospel According to Mark* (Cambridge, England: Cambridge University Press, 1963), 5–6; A. M. Hunter, *The Gospel According to St. Mark* (London: SCM Press, 1953), 16–17; Robert M. Grant, *An Historical Introduction to the New Testament* (London: Collins, 1963), 119; F. F. Bruce, *The New Testament Documents*, rev. ed. (Grand Rapids, MI: Eerdmans, 1960), 35–37; R. A. Cole, *The Gospel According to St. Mark* (Grand Rapids, MI: Eerdmans, 1970), 28–50; Everett F. Harrison, *Introduction to the New Testament* (Grand Rapids, MI: Eerdmans, 1964), 174–175.

5. Norval Geldenhuys, *Commentary on the Gospel of Luke* (Grand Rapids, MI: Eerdmans, 1972), 15–22; E. J. Tinsley, *The Gospel According to Luke* (Cambridge, England: Cambridge University Press, 1965), 2–4; C. F. D. Moule, *Christ's Messengers: Studies in Acts of the Apostles* (New York: Association Press, 1957), 10–13; A. M. Hunter, *Introducing the New Testament*, 2nd ed. (Philadelphia: Westminster Press, 1957), especially 49–50; William Hamilton, *The Modern Reader's Guide to Matthew and Luke* (New York: Association Press, 1957), 14; Robert Grant, *Historical Introduction to New Testament*, 134–135; F. F. Bruce, *Commentary on the Book of Acts* (Grand Rapids, MI: Eerdmans, 1971), 19; Ray Summers, *Commentary on Luke* (Waco, TX: Word Books, 1972), 8–10; Harrison, *Introduction to the New Testament*, 185–191, 223–225.

6. Hunter, *Introducing the New Testament*, 55–56; Grant, *Historical Introduction to New Testament*, 129; Bruce, *The New Testament Documents*, 39–40; Ned B. Stonehouse, *Origins of the Synoptic Gospels* (Grand Rapids, MI: Eerdmans, 1963), 43–47; C. Stewart Petrie, "The Authorship of 'The Gospel According to Matthew': A Reconsideration of the External Evidence," in *New Testament Studies*, vol. 14, October 1967, 15–33; Harrison, *Introduction to the New Testament*, 166–167.

7. Raymond Brown, *The Gospel According to John* (Garden City, NY: Doubleday, 1966), 87–104; Leon Morris, *The Gospel According to John* (Grand Rapids, MI: Eerdmans, 1971), 8–35; R. V. G. Tasker, *The Gospel According to St. John* (Grand Rapids, MI: Eerdmans, 1968), 11–20; Hunter, *Introducing the New Testament*, 61–63; Grant, *Historical Introduction to New Testament*, 160; William Hamilton, *The Modern Reader's Guide to John* (New York: Association Press, 1959), 13–15; John A. T. Robinson, *Can We Trust*

the New Testament? (Grand Rapids, MI: Eerdmans, 1977), 83; Bruce, *The New Testament Documents,* 48–49; Harrison, *Introduction to the New Testament,* 207–214.

8. As an example of his distrust of the Gospel's historicity, Professor Pannenberg questions my acceptance of Jesus' predictions of his Resurrection. In *The Resurrection of Jesus* (Grand Rapids, MI: Baker Book House, 1980), I present three arguments in favor of the historicity of these predictions (pp. 63–67). Others who accept the historicity of these predictions include Cullmann, *The Christology of the New Testament,* rev. ed., trans. Shirley Hall and Charles Hall (Philadelphia: Westminster Press, 1963), 63; Ladd, *I Believe in the Resurrection of Jesus* (Grand Rapids, MI: Eerdmans, 1975), 35–36, 70–72; and Murray Harris, *Raised Immortal: Resurrection and Immortality in the New Testament* (Grand Rapids, MI: Eerdmans, 1983), 8, 12.

9. Sherwin-White, *Roman Society and Roman Law in the New Testament* (Oxford: Oxford University Press, 1963; Grand Rapids, MI: Baker Book House, 1978), 189–190.

10. *Ibid.,* 187–191.

11. See especially *Ibid.,* 186–193, and Michael Grant, *Jesus: An Historian's Review of the Gospels* (New York: Scribner, 1977) 180–184.

12. Robert M. Price, "Is There a Place for Historical Criticism?" (Paper delivered in a debate on "The Historical Foundations of Christianity," in Dallas, Texas, February 9, 1985). Interestingly, Price (who represented the atheistic-skeptical position) admitted that there is a historical core in spite of legend (20, 24) and even stated in the debate dialogue that the Gospels are generally reliable texts.

13. Sherwin-White, *Roman Society and Roman Law,* 190. Cf. Grant, *Jesus,* p. 182.

14. Dodd, "The Appearances of the Risen Christ: An Essay in Form-Criticism of the Gospels," in *More New Testament Studies* (Grand Rapids, MI: Eerdmans, 1968).

15. Edward Lynn Bode, *The First Easter Morning,* Analecta Biblica 45 (Rome: Biblical Institute Press, 1970) 155–175; William Lane Craig, "The Empty Tomb of Jesus," in *Gospel Perspectives: Studies of History and Tradition in the Four Gospels,* vol. 2, ed. R. T. France and David Wenham (Sheffield, England: JSOT Press, 1981), 173–200; Robert H. Stein, "Was the Tomb Really Empty?" *Journal of the Evangelical Theological Society* 20:1 (March 1977): 23–29.

16. This view is taught in several Jewish writings that influenced the first century, such as 2 Maccabees 14:46 (cf. 7:9, 12:43–45); the Apocalypse of Baruch 50:2–51:10; and 1 Enoch 51:1–2, 62:13–16. This is not to imply that other beliefs were not taught by some (see Wisdom of Solomon 2:23, 3:1–10 and 5 Enoch 103:4).

17. This does not include subjective claims of hallucination, which have been addressed repeatedly in the debate and dialogue.

18. This is the most likely explanation of Acts 9:7 and 22:9. The former uses the genitive, indicating the hearing of sounds, and the latter uses the accusative, indicating hearing with understanding. For details, see Robertson, *Word Pictures in the New Testament* (Nashville: Broadman Press, 1930), vol. III, p. 390.

19. See William Lane Craig, "The Bodily Resurrection of Jesus" in *Gospel Perspectives: Studies of History and Tradition in the Four Gospels,* vol. 1, ed. R. T. France and David Wenham (Sheffield, England: JSOT Press, 1980), 51.

20. Pannenberg, *Jesus—God and Man,* trans. Lewis L. Wilkens and Duane A. Priebe (Philadelphia: Westminster Press, 1968), 92–93, for example.

21. See Bode, *The First Easter Morning,* 93–96, for a study of this issue.

22. Luke 24:34, 39; John 20:20, 25, and so on.
23. *The Interpreter's Dictionary of the Bible,* four volumes, ed. George A. Buttrick (Nashville: Abingdon Press, 1962), s.v. "Resurrection in the N.T." by John A. T. Robinson, vol. 4, 47–48.
24. Craig, "The Bodily Resurrection of Jesus," 58.
25. Harris, *Raised Immortal,* 53.
26. *Ibid.,* 57; cf. 147.
27. See Matt. 16:17, Gal. 1:16, Eph. 6:12, and Heb. 2:14.
28. Craig, "The Bodily Resurrection of Jesus," 64; cf. 60, 69.
29. Harris, *Raised Immortal,* 118; cf. 119.
30. *Ibid.,* 217.
31. Robinson, "Resurrection in the N.T.," 48.
32. For major, relevant studies, see John A. T. Robinson, *The Body: A Study in Pauline Theology* (Philadelphia: Westminster Press, 1952); Robert H. Gundry, *Soma in Biblical Theology* (Cambridge, England: Cambridge University Press, 1976).
33. Strauss, *A New Life of Jesus* (London: Williams and Norgate, 1879), vol. 1, 412.
34. For a more in depth response, see Habermas, *Ancient Evidence for the Life of Jesus,* 54–58.
35. Schweitzer, *The Quest of the Historical Jesus,* trans. W. Montgomery (New York: Macmillan, 1906; reprint, 1968).
36. Eduard Riggenbach, *The Resurrection of Jesus* (New York: Eaton and Mains, 1907), 48–49; James Orr, *The Resurrection of Jesus* (1908; reprint, Grand Rapids, MI: Zondervan Publishing House, 1965), 92.
37. For a critique of this opinion, see Habermas, *Ancient Evidence for the Life of Jesus,* 31–36. The rejections of this theory by Price, "Is There a Place for Historical Criticism?," 19–20 and Grant, *Jesus: An Historian's Review of the Gospels,* 199–200 are quite instructional in view of the approaches of these two critical scholars.
38. Sherwin-White, *Roman Society and Roman Law in the New Testament,* 186–191; Michael Grant, *Jesus,* 182, 184.
39. Charles Hartshorne, *Omnipotence and Other Theological Mistakes* (Albany: State University of New York, 1984), 32–37.
40. For a brief overview of numerous such arguments, see Peter Kreeft, "The Case for Life After Death," *Truth* 1 (1985): 107–111.
41. See Habermas, *The Resurrection of Jesus,* for details of this argument.
42. For some of the relevant works, see Karlis Osis and Erlendur Haraldsson, *At the Hour of Death* (New York: Avon Books, 1977); John Audette, "Denver Cardiologist Discloses Findings After 18 Years of Near-Death Research," *Anabiosis* 1 (1979): 1–2; Kenneth Ring, *Life At Death: A Scientific Investigation of the Near-Death Experience* (New York: Coward, McCann and Geoghegan, 1980); Dina Ingber, "Visions of an Afterlife," in *Science Digest* 89:1 (January–February, 1981): 94–97, 142; Michael Sabom, *Recollections of Death: A Medical Investigation* (New York: Harper & Row, 1982).
43. Personal conversation with Antony Flew, May 6, 1985.
44. Although details have not been argued here, see Habermas, *The Resurrection of Jesus,* 155–162.
45. On the meaningfulness of heaven, see Peter Kreeft, *Heaven: The Heart's Deepest Longing* (San Francisco: Harper & Row, 1980).

46. For argumentation relative to each of these points, see Habermas, *The Resurrection of Jesus.*

47. See Stevenson and Habermas, *Verdict on the Shroud,* (Ann Arbor, MI: Servant Books, 1981; Wayne, PA: Dell, 1982), Part II, "Conclusions from the Facts," for some groundwork that we did before entertaining any notions about the cause of the image.

48. *Ibid.,* especially Part II, "Conclusions from the Facts," and 191–193; John Heller, *Report on the Shroud of Turin* (Boston: Houghton Mifflin, 1983).

49. See Gary R. Habermas, "The Shroud of Turin: A Rejoinder to Basinger and Basinger," *Journal of the Evangelical Theological Society,* 25:2 (June 1982), 219–227, as well as the other articles in this debate that are published in this issue.

50. Details are provided in Habermas, *The Resurrection of Jesus,* Part One, "A Resurrection Apologetic: Five Steps," in particular.

SELECT BIBLIOGRAPHY

Anderson, J. N. D. *The Evidence for the Resurrection.* Downers Grove, IL: Inter-Varsity Press, 1966.

————. "The Resurrection of Jesus Christ." *Christianity Today* (March 29, 1968).

Anderson, J. N. D., Lawrence Burkholder, Harvey Cox, and Wolfhart Pannenberg. "A Dialogue on Christ's Resurrection." *Christianity Today* (April 12, 1968).

Barth, Karl. *The Resurrection of the Dead.* Translated by H. J. Stenning. New York: Revell, 1933.

————. "The Doctrine of Reconciliation." In *Church Dogmatics.* Vol. 4, Part 1. Edited by G. W. Bromiley and T. F. Torrence. Edinburgh, Scotland: T. and T. Clark, 1956.

Barth, Markus, Leonhard Goppelt, Helmut Thielicke, and H. R. Mullerschwefe. *The Easter Message Today.* New York: Nelson, 1964.

Barth, Markus, and Verne H. Fletcher. *Acquittal by Resurrection.* New York: Holt, Rinehart & Winston, 1964.

Benoit, P. *Passion et Resurrection du Seigneur.* Paris: Cerf, 1966.

Bode, Edward Lynn. *The First Easter Morning.* Analecta Biblica 45. Rome: Biblical Institute Press, 1970.

Brown, Raymond E. "The Resurrection and Biblical Criticism." *Commonweal* 24 (1967): 232–236.

————. *The Virginal Conception and Bodily Resurrection of Jesus.* New York: Paulist Press, 1973.

Cerfaux, Lucien. *Christ in the Theology of St. Paul.* New York: Herder and Herder, 1966.

Clark, Neville. *Interpreting the Resurrection.* London: SCM Press, 1967.

Craig, William Lane. "The Bodily Resurrection of Jesus." In *Gospel Perspectives I.* Edited by R. T. France and David Wenham. Sheffield, England: JSOT Press, 1980.

————. "The Empty Tomb." In *Gospel Perspectives II.* Edited by R. T. France and David Wenham. Sheffield, England: JSOT Press, 1981.

————. *The Son Rises: Historical Evidence for the Resurrection of Jesus.* Chicago: Moody, 1981.

————. *The Historical Argument for the Resurrection of Jesus During the Deist Controversy.* Toronto, Canada: Edwin Mellen, 1985.

Cullmann, Oscar. *Immortality of the Soul or Resurrection of the Dead?* New York: Macmillan, 1958.

Dodd, C. H. "The Appearances of the Risen Christ." In *Studies in the Gospels.* Oxford, 1955, 15–16, 31–33.

Dulles, Avery. *Apologetics and the Biblical Christ.* Philadelphia,: Westminster Press, 1967.

Durrwell, F. X. *The Resurrection: A Biblical Study.* New York: Sheed & Ward, 1960.

Flew, Antony G. N. "Miracles and Methodology." In *Hume's Philosophy of Belief.* London: Routledge and Kegan Paul, 1961.

———. "The Credentials of Revelation: Miracle and History." In *God and Philosophy.* New York: Dell, 1966.

———. "Miracles." In *Encyclopedia of Philosophy.* Edited by Paul Edwards. New York: Macmillan and the Free Press, 1967.

———. Introduction to David Hume's *Of Miracles.* La Salle, IL: Open Court, 1985.

Fuller, Daniel P. *Easter Faith and History.* Grand Rapids, MI: Eerdmans, 1965.

Fuller, Reginald H. *The Formation of the Resurrection Narratives.* New York: Macmillan, 1971.

Grass, Hans. *Ostergeschehen und Osterberichte.* Göttingen, W. Germany: Bandenhoed und Ruprecht, 1962.

Green, Michael. *Man Alive!* Downers Grove, IL: Inter-Varsity Press, 1967.

———. *The Empty Cross of Jesus.* Downers Grove, IL: Inter-Varsity Press, 1984.

Habermas, Gary R. *The Resurrection of Jesus: A Rational Inquiry.* Ann Arbor, MI: University Microfilms, 1976.

———. *The Resurrection of Jesus: An Apologetic.* Grand Rapids, MI: Baker Book House, 1980.

———. *Ancient Evidence for the Life of Jesus: Historical Records of His Death and Resurrection.* New York: Nelson, 1984.

Habermas, Gary R., and Kenneth E. Stevenson. *Verdict on the Shroud: Evidence for the Death and Resurrection of Jesus Christ.* Ann Arbor, MI: Servant Books, 1981.

Haes, J. de. *La Résurrection de Jesus dans l'apologetique des cinquante dernieres annees.* Rome: 1953.

Harris, Murray J. *Raised Immortal: Resurrection and Immortality in the New Testament.* Grand Rapids, MI: Eerdmans, 1983.

Jansen, John Frederick. *The Resurrection of Jesus Christ in New Testament Theology.* Philadelphia: Westminster Press, 1980.

Kennedy, John. *The Resurrection of Jesus.* London: Religious Tract Society, 1881.

Koch, Gerhard. *Die Auferstehung Jesu Christi.* Tübingen, W. Germany: J. C. B. Mohr, 1959.

Kunneth, Walter. *The Theology of the Resurrection.* St. Louis: Concordia, 1965.

Ladd, George Eldon. *I Believe in the Resurrection of Jesus.* Grand Rapids, MI: Eerdmans, 1975.

Lampe, G. W. H., and D. M. MacKinnon. *The Resurrection: A Dialogue.* Philadelphia: Westminster Press, 1966.

Lapide, Pinchas. *The Resurrection of Jesus: A Jewish Perspective.* Minneapolis, MN: Augsburg, 1983.

Leaney, A. R. C. "The Resurrection Narratives in Luke 24:12–53." *New Testament Studies* 2 (1955–1956): 110–114.

Lewis, C. S. *Miracles.* New York: Macmillan, 1947.

Loane, M. L. *Our Risen Lord.* Grand Rapids, MI: Zondervan, 1965.

Marxsen, Willi. *Die Auferstehung Jesu als historisches und als theologisches Problem.* W. Germany: Gutersloh, 1966.

————. *The Resurrection of Jesus of Nazareth.* Translated by Margaret Kohl. Philadelphia: Fortress Press, 1970.

Milligan, William. *The Resurrection of Our Lord.* London: Macmillan, 1884.

Moltmann, Jurgan. *Theology of Hope.* Translated by James W. Leitch. New York: Harper & Row, 1967.

Montgomery, J. W. *History and Christianity.* Downers Grove, IL: Inter-Varsity Press, 1965.

Morison, Frank. *Who Moved the Stone?* Grand Rapids, MI: Zondervan, 1958.

Moule, C.F.D. "The Post-Resurrection Appearances." *New Testament Studies* 4 (1957–1958): 61.

Moule, C. F. D., ed. *The Significance of the Message of the Resurrection for Faith in Jesus Christ.* London: SCM Press, 1968.

Mussner, Franz. *Die Auferstehung Jesu.* Munich: Kosel-Verlag, 1969.

Niebuhr, Richard. *Resurrection and Historical Reason.* New York: Scribner, 1957.

O'Collins, Gerald. *What Are They Saying About the Resurrection?* New York: Paulist Press, 1978.

O'Donovan, Oliver. *Resurrection and Moral Order.* Grand Rapids, MI: Eerdmans, 1986.

Osborne, Grant. *The Resurrection Narratives: A Redactional Study.* Grand Rapids, MI: Baker Book House, 1984.

Orr, James. *The Resurrection of Jesus.* Grand Rapids, MI: Zondervan, 1965.

Pannenberg, Wolfhart. *Jesus—God and Man.* Translated by Lewis L. Wilkens and Duane Priebe. Philadelphia: Westminster Press, 1968.

————, ed. *Revelation as History.* Translated by David Granskou. London: Macmillan, 1968.

Perkins, Pheme. *Resurrection: New Testament Witness and Contemporary Reflection.* New York: Doubleday, 1984.

Perrin, Norman. *The Resurrection According to Matthew, Mark and Luke.* Philadelphia: Fortress Press, 1977.

Ramsey, A. M. *The Resurrection of Christ.* London: Geoffrey Bless, 1962.

Rigaux, B. "L'Historicite de Jesus Devant L'Exegese Recente." *Revue Biblique* (1958): 481–522.

Riggenbach, Eduard. *The Resurrection of Jesus.* New York: Eaton and Mains, 1907.

Russel, R. "Modern Exegesis and the Fact of the Resurrection." *Downside Review* 76 (1958): 25–64, 329–343.

Sider, Ronald J. "The Pauline Conception of the Resurrection Body in I Corinthians XV. 35–54." *New Testament Studies* 21 428–439.

————. "St. Paul's Understanding of the Nature and Significance of the Resurrection in I Corinthians XV 1;19." *Novum Testamentum* 19 (1977): 124–141.

Smith, Wilber. "Scientists and the Resurrection." *Christianity Today* (April 15, 1957).

Sparrow-Simpson, W. J. *Our Lord's Resurrection.* Grand Rapids, MI: Zondervan, 1964.

Sparrow-Simpson, W. J. *The Resurrection and the Christian Faith.* Grand Rapids, MI: Zondervan, 1968.

Tannehill, Robert C. *Dying and Rising with Christ.* Berlin: Topelmann, 1967.

Tenney, Merrill C. *The Reality of the Resurrection.* New York: Harper & Row, 1963.

————. *The Vital Heart of Christianity.* Grand Rapids, MI: Zondervan, 1964.

Torrance, Thomas. *Space, Time and Resurrection.* Grand Rapids, MI: Eerdmans, 1976.

Ulrich, Wilckens. *Resurrection. Biblical Testimony to the Resurrection: An Historical Examination and Explanation.* Translated by A. M. Stewart. Edinburgh, Scotland: Saint Andrew Press, 1977.

Vawter, Bruce. "Resurrection and Redemption." *Catholic Biblical Quarterly* (1953): 11–23.

Wenham, John. *Easter Enigma: Are the Resurrection Accounts in Conflict?* Grand Rapids, MI: Zondervan, 1984.

CONTRIBUTOR BIOGRAPHIES

PARTICIPANTS IN THE DEBATE

GARY R. HABERMAS is professor of apologetics and philosophy at Liberty University and Director of Liberty's Master's program in Apologetics. Dr. Habermas holds the B.R.E. from *William Tyndale College*, the M.A. from the *University of Detroit*, and the Ph.D. from *Michigan State University*. Dr. Habermas has written four other books on the Resurrection: *The Resurrection of Jesus: A Rational Inquiry, The Resurrection of Jesus: An Apologetic, Verdict on the Shroud: Evidence for the Death and Resurrection of Jesus Christ,* and most recently, *Ancient Evidence for the Life of Jesus: Historical Records of His Death and Resurrection* (Nashville: Thomas Nelson Publishers, 1984). He has also written numerous articles.

ANTONY G. N. FLEW was for many years professor of philosophy at the University of Reading, England. Before this Dr. Flew taught at Christ Church, University of Oxford; King's College, University of Aberdeen; and the University of Keele. He has also been a visiting professor at twelve universities around the world. Dr. Flew holds the M.A. from *St. John's College, University of Oxford,* and a D.Lit. from the *University of Keele.* Dr. Flew has written sixteen books. Among the most famous are *God and Philosophy, The Presumption of Atheism,* and most recently, *David Hume: Philosopher of Social Science* (Oxford: Blackwell's, 1985). Dr. Flew has also edited nine books and written dozens of articles.

TERRY L. MIETHE is dean of the Oxford Study Centre, Oxford, England, professor of philosophy at Liberty University, and an adjunct professor at Wycliffe Hall, Oxford. Before this Dr. Miethe taught at Saint Louis University and the University of Southern California. He has also been a visiting professor at seven colleges and universities around the world. Dr. Miethe holds the M.A. from *Trinity Evangelical Divinity School;* the M.Div. from *McCormick Theological Seminary;* the Ph.D. in philosophy, Phi Beta Kappa, from *Saint Louis University;* and an A.M. and Ph.D. in social ethics from the *University of Southern California.* Dr. Miethe has written seven books, including works on Augustine and Aquinas, and most recently, *The New Christian's Guide to Following Jesus* (Minneapolis: Bethany House Publishers, 1984) and *The Christian's Guide to Faith and Reason* (Minneapolis: Bethany House, 1987). He has also written numerous articles.

W. DAVID BECK is director of Graduate Studies, School of Religion; chair of the Department of Philosophy; and professor of philosophy at Liberty University. Dr. Beck holds the B.A. from *Houghton College,* the M.A. from *Trinity Evangelical Divinity School,* and the Ph.D. from *Boston University.* Dr. Beck has contributed to several anthologies, including *Principalities and Powers,* edited by J. W. Montgomery, and *Biblical Errancy: An Analysis of Its Philosophical Roots,* edited by N. L. Geisler.

RESPONDENTS TO THE DEBATE

WOLFHART PANNENBERG is professor of systematic theology at the University of Munich. Dr. Pannenberg studied at *Basel University, Heidelberg University,* and *Göttingen.* He has written eleven books, including *The Idea of God and Human Freedom, Jesus —God and Man,* and *Theology and the Philosophy of Science,* and dozens of articles. Dr. Pannenberg is the subject of two volumes: one in the *Makers of the Modern Theological Mind* series entitled *Wolfhart Pannenberg* by Don H. Olive (Waco, TX: Word, 1987) and one by E. Frank Tupper, *The Theology of Wolfhart Pannenberg* (Philadelphia: Westminister, 1987).

CHARLES HARTSHORNE was for many years professor of philosophy at The University of Texas at Austin. He holds the A.B., A.M., and Ph.D. from *Harvard University.* Dr. Hartshorne taught at The University of Chicago and Emory University before coming to Texas and has held visiting professorships around the world. Dr. Hartshorne has written ten books, among them *Anselm's Discovery: A Re-examination of the Ontological Proof for God's Existence* and *Creative Synthesis and Philosophic Method,* and numerous articles. Dr. Hartshorne is the subject of a volume in the *Makers of the Modern Theological Mind* series entitled *Charles Hartshorne* (Waco, TX: Word 1973) by Alan Gragg.

JAMES I. PACKER is professor of historical and systematic theology at Regent College in Vancouver, British Columbia. Before this Dr. Packer was associate principal of Trinity College, Bristol, England. Dr. Packer holds the M.A. from *Corpus Christi College, University of Oxford;* his training for the ministry in the Anglican church was at *Wycliffe Hall, Oxford;* and he holds the D.Phil. from the *University of Oxford.* He is the author of several books, including *Knowing God, Evangelism and the Sovereignty of God, God Has Spoken,* and *God Speaks to Man.* Dr. Packer is the subject of a chapter in *Five Evangelical Leaders* by Christopher Catherwood (London: Hodder and Stoughton, 1984).